Sunset

ideas for great
GREAT ROOMS

By Barbara J. Braasch and
the Editors of Sunset Books

Sunset Books ■ Menlo Park, California

Sunset Books

vice president, general manager:
Richard A. Smeby

vice president, editorial director:
Bob Doyle

production director:
Lory Day

director of operations:
Rosann Sutherland

art director:
Vasken Guiragossian

Staff for this book:

developmental editor:
Linda J. Selden

copy editor:
Phyllis Elving

photo director/stylist:
JoAnn Masaoka Van Atta

principal photographer:
E. Andrew McKinney

design:
Barbara Vick

page layout:
Susan Bryant Caron

production coordinator:
Eligio Hernandez

proofreader:
Mary Roybal

10 9 8 7 6 5 4 3 2 1
First printing June 2002

ISBN 0-376-01249-8
Library of Congress Control Number: 2001094597
Printed in the United States.

For additional copies of Ideas for Great Great Rooms or any other Sunset book, see our web site at www.sunsetbooks.com or call 1-800-526-5111.

Cover: Raising the ceiling, adding a wall of glass, and opening the kitchen to the living-dining area transformed separate small, dark spaces into one light-filled great room—without adding square footage. Design: Ann Beeman Architects. Cover design by Vasken Guiragossian. Photography by Alex Hayden.

Below: A step up from the fireplace's extended hearth takes an entertainment unit to a whole new level. Title page: Washed in warm colors and good lighting, a contemporary great room boasts treetop views.

Gathering places & welcoming spaces

As your family grows or as it shrinks, with singles striking out on their own, you may discover a need to reconfigure your home. Maybe you want more rooms, or perhaps existing rooms are now available for new purposes. A home that holds its own through the revolving door of change is a true treasure, a place where family and friends can always feel welcome.

This book takes a close look at a home's public space, the place where family members gather for dining, talking, listening to music, watching television, and entertaining guests. Often it's a great room, that multipurpose space that may serve as kitchen, dining room, and living room in one open area. Or it may be the more traditional family room or family kitchen, an action-oriented recreation room, a state-of-the-art media center, or even a sun-drenched garden room.

On the following pages, you'll find many bright ideas for reorganizing, redesigning, or even completely remodeling your home's gathering space. Photographs throughout this book concentrate on rooms with inventive spaces and unique profiles to inspire you. For the names of architects and designers whose work is featured, turn to pages 126–127.

contents

ROOMS FOR ALL REASONS

GREAT ROOMS, FAMILY ROOMS, and even family kitchens are variations on the same theme: they are all gathering spaces designed to be used for more than one purpose. Whether folks get together here for cooking and eating, socializing with family and friends, watching television, listening to music, or playing games, these rooms shine when the gang's all here. UNIFYING AREAS where so many disparate activities take place can be a real challenge, but in the pages of this book we'll show you how other people have altered their houses to do just that. THE FRESH IDEAS presented here can help you transform a not-so-fulfilling space in your own home into the one special place where your family truly lives.

Great rooms

What is a great room? Ask people who have one and they'll tell you it's the most lived-in part of a modern home. Designed to be shared by family and friends, a great room often includes kitchen, dining, and living functions in areas that are physically and visually open to each other. Activity zones flow together rather than being completely separated by walls.

The idea dates back to colonial days, when a family lived, slept, cooked, ate, and entertained in one large space—often sharing the area with their livestock. Though sleeping now takes place in another part of the home and livestock is relegated elsewhere, today's great room is very much in keeping with the old tradition.

This open and airy space not only serves family members, but it also provides an ideal entertaining area. Often the great room boasts a broad expanse of windows offering panoramic views or glass doors opening onto a deck or terrace.

Comfortable seating areas foster conversation, and when it's time for hors d'oeuvres, a nearby dining table means they may be enjoyed without moving to another room.

Great rooms should be welcoming day and night, with sunlight streaming in through windows or skylights and interior lighting setting a mood as well as defining separate areas within the room. In a space where so much activity takes place, storage is very important, too. A great room benefits from built-in or freestanding cabinets, bookshelves, and drawers.

Opening up smaller rooms to make one large open space usually involves removing walls and defining separate activity areas instead by means of arches, columns, alcoves, or varied floor or ceiling levels. But sometimes just changing floor coverings or adding rugs is enough to mark where one activity area ends and the next one begins.

Varying widely in design and decor, these two great rooms share such important features as comfort and convenience. And both make the most of their space with plenty of built-in storage.

This high-beamed family room offers plenty of space to play or curl up and read. Built-in shelves at both ends of the window seat hold books.

Family rooms and family kitchens

The great room's more modest cousin is the family room. Though it is often situated off the kitchen, no cooking takes place in the family room itself. This is probably a home's most comfortable spot, the place where family members gather to watch television or share other forms of entertainment. Guests may be entertained more formally in a separate living room.

The kitchen is a popular gathering space in its own right. To allow more room for chatting and eating, many of today's family kitchens have been expanded to include a dining area—an island with stools, a kitchen table, or perhaps both—that provides limited space for informal meals and socializing. If there's room for a small seating area as well, guests can converse in comfort without getting in the cook's way.

Private spaces

Just as families differ, the way they use their homes differs, too. Sometimes the very openness of a great room may make it desirable to dedicate part of your layout as a quiet place to read, watch television, listen to music, or just talk with a friend. Let another space handle crowds—private places are the perfect spots for a favorite chair, a good reading lamp, some books, and perhaps a desk for sorting through mail.

As modern life becomes ever more complicated, many families find the need for an office space set apart from the main gathering area of their home. Connected to the open area with screens, pocket doors, or French doors, this work area can be separate and private when closed off; when the doors or screens are opened, it's part of the loop of family activity.

Built-ins are particularly well suited to such private retreats. Not only do they allow you to tailor space to your specific needs, but they also lend a more formal, businesslike appearance to an area that is to be used as a home office, either occasionally or on a full-time basis.

Tucked into a nook of a multipurpose room, an inviting personal space allows you to welcome a friend for coffee and a little private conversation.

DEFINING YOUR SPACE

I**T'S OFFICIAL**. Surveys by the National Association of Home Builders confirm that the formal living room, like the little-used Victorian parlor, is nearing extinction. Today's families are looking for a more casual, do-everything gathering place, where they can chat with the cook, entertain guests, pay bills, go online, screen movies, do homework, or just relax. Great room, family room, or fusion space—no matter what you call it, it's the heart of the home, the place where we really live.

USE THIS CHAPTER of practical ideas as a starting point to help you come up with a fresh, open plan that suits your family's lifestyle. We'll help you evaluate your existing home, guide you through layout and design basics, show you what's involved in the art of the remodel, and explain how designers and contractors can help you realize your dreams.

a family profile

LIKE TO KEEP AN EYE *on the kids while cooking? Want to curl up on a window seat with a good book or bask in a sunroom? Before you start tearing down walls and rearranging rooms to fulfill those dreams, you'll want to take stock of what you have—and determine how you will reconcile your dreams and your budget.*

Dreams versus reality

An analysis of how your existing rooms are used will probably surprise you. It will certainly offer a new look at your family's lifestyle.

Begin by listing each room in your house, along with its approximate square footage. List the activities that take place in each room, how often they occur, and who does them. Then organize your list from most-used to least-used rooms. You probably will notice that some large rooms receive little use, a clear indication that you may want to rework that space.

Another helpful tool—and one that's fun to make—is a wish list of all the ideas you have for a new gathering place. Even if many items appear to be way beyond your budget, include everything that family members feel would give them pleasure, from a playroom to a movie theater. Be as specific as possible, adding any illustrations you may have collected.

When your wish list is complete, identify which "wants" are definite "musts," which would be nice but could be omitted if cost prohibits, and which are completely in the realm of fantasy. Then make a second list, describing the "musts" in more detail. Add whatever would be necessary to make your gathering space work the way you want it to, such as new storage, lighting, or furniture. You have now created a reality list, a framework for setting goals to create the home you envision.

Budgeting for size and style

Before you hire a designer or pick up a sledge-hammer, consider your budget. Altering living

Replacing a load-bearing wall with a structural beam unites a small sitting area (left) and the kitchen (below) in a single airy space that lets the chef keep an eye on both the meal and family or guests. On the facing page, a kitchen gains built-in seating and generous storage space with the addition of a simple bay.

space often pits dreams against realities. To reconcile the two, you need to consider three variables—cost, quantity, and quality. In any design change, two of the three factors can remain constant, but the third has to be adjustable.

Allowing cost to be a variable, if you have that luxury, offers the greatest flexibility in terms of dream fulfillment. By increasing the size of your project (quantity) or the level of detailing (quality), you increase cost. But how big does your new space really have to be? Many people opt for as large a space as possible; after all, that's probably what prompted a redesign in the first place. If your vision has little to do with size, however, the quality of the space might be improved by reducing square footage. By using a simpler, not-so-large plan, you can enrich the quality of your space, adding higher-grade materials and special detailing.

exploring your options

AS WE ALL KNOW, *homes were different a century ago, with structured rooms that reflected a more formal way of life. The concept of open living spaces didn't emerge until the 1950s. First, living rooms and dining rooms were blended. Then a separate room was introduced to house that epoch's new marvel, the television.*

Many of us still live in houses with poorly configured floor plans and no all-purpose room where the family can get together. Even if your house was once a perfect fit for your family, your present lifestyle is probably fundamentally different from what it used to be. As a family grows and changes through the years, its home needs to keep pace.

Tailoring your space so that it's more in sync with the way you live today may be easier than you imagine, thanks to new materials, simpler installation techniques, and creative open-space planning.

When thinking of changing or adding space, it's wise to consider both what you need today and what you will need in the future. A desire for more space is often the paramount reason for altering a residence. But new interests, new occupations, and new technology may also act as spurs for conversions. Maybe you would like a place to screen movies or listen to audio equipment. If you work out of your home, configuring space to add office equipment may make good sense.

Fortunate is the family who can transform its home by simple redecoration. Most people need to at least rework space. Often, minor adjustments can solve problems. Adding more light by enlarging existing windows, for example, can make a room seem larger and more inviting. Building a window seat with drawers underneath increases both storage space and seating capacity.

Look around your home for space you might not have thought of before. If your dining room is used only on holidays, you might be able to convert it into a family room and connect it to the kitchen by knocking out a wall or two. Perhaps a rarely used breakfast room can be converted into a combination greenhouse/sunroom. Add window walls, bring in plants, and replace kitchen table and chairs with comfortable wicker furniture and you've turned your underutilized space into a charming spot to entertain family and guests.

Converting an existing space requires fewer structural changes than building an addition. Sometimes you can make rooms flow into one another simply by widening arches between them. Often the way to unify space is to rearrange rooms, remove walls, or raise ceilings. Knocking down walls between kitchen, dining room, and living room can create an all-purpose great room. Transforming a back porch into a sunroom or converting an attached garage into a family room are relatively easy and inexpensive ways to access space.

French doors connect a remodeled kitchen and breakfast room with the home's new rear terrace, visually "stretching" the interior space into the outdoors and offering diners an alfresco experience.

a room redux

MANY HOMES *are veritable gold mines of underutilized space that can be drafted into service or, as in the case of a garage or porch, changed from one use to another. Whether you do it yourself or hire professional help, changing your home's structure will require extensive work. Check with your local building department for applicable codes and permits.*

Structural changes

If you're planning to open up space, add a skylight or window wall, or lay a heavy stone floor, your house may require structural modifications. As shown below, walls are either bearing (supporting the weight of the ceiling joists and/or second-story walls) or nonbearing. If you're removing all or part of a bearing wall, you must bridge the gap with a sturdy beam and posts. Nonbearing ("partition") walls usually can be removed without too much trouble, unless pipes or wires are routed through them.

Doors and windows require special framing, as illustrated; the required header size depends on the width of the opening and your local building codes. Skylights require similar cuts through ceiling joists and/or rafters. Planning a vaulted or cathedral ceiling instead of your present ceiling? You'll probably need to install a few beams to maintain structural soundness.

Hardwood, ceramic tile, and stone floors require very stiff underlayment. You can solve the problem by beefing up the floor joists and/or adding plywood or particleboard subflooring on top of the existing floor.

Expanding into the garage

Converting an adjoining garage into a family room—or into a quiet media room or home office off a gathering room—is a relatively easy task. The garage is easily accessible, it's located at ground level, and it offers a large, unobstructed space. Electricity is probably already available, with water and heat not far away, although insulation may be needed.

STRUCTURAL FRAMING

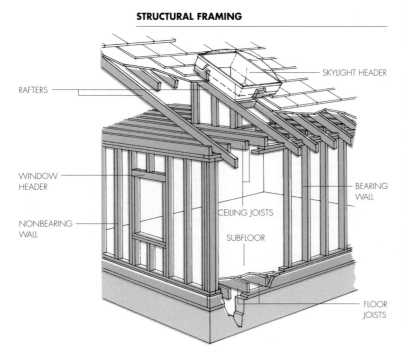

RAFTERS

SKYLIGHT HEADER

WINDOW HEADER

NONBEARING WALL

CEILING JOISTS

SUBFLOOR

BEARING WALL

FLOOR JOISTS

Annexing an adjacent two-car garage created a spacious gathering place (left) off the kitchen. Columns, a low wall, and a modest change in floor level define cooking, dining, and seating areas. The breakfast table (below) shares views of the television and the fireplace with the seating area.

A major concern is what to do with the garage door. You will probably want to remove it and frame in the wall, taking advantage of this opportunity to introduce windows or glass doors. For more information, consult the Sunset book *Converting Garages, Attics & Basements*.

With landscaping and a little carpentry, you can re-create an exterior that looks more like an extension of the house than a storage depot for mowers and Mazdas. Check local building codes before banishing the car, though; in many areas, covered spaces must be provided for cars.

Converting a porch or patio

Turning a framed porch into an extra room may be as simple as adding windows and, if not already installed, lighting and heat. Patio conversion is much more difficult; if the foundation does not meet building codes, you'll virtually be starting from scratch. This may turn out to be as much work as adding an entirely new room.

defining your space

HOME THEATER BASICS

A home sound system can range from a traditional stereo with built-in speakers to a complete surround-sound system tied to a big-screen television. What your family needs depends on its musical and viewing interests, the size and arrangement of your house, and your budget. You can install a multiroom sound system that controls music from several locations around the house. Some sophisticated sound systems include telephone and security functions.

What transforms television, VCR, sound system, and other black boxes into a formal home theater is the relationship between these devices, all tied together with low-voltage wires and cables. So if your family gathers around the electronic hearth to watch television, or if you plan a separate media room, you have to consider how to place and wire your audio and video equipment.

You'll need a special A/V receiver to drive the five or more speakers in your viewing room. If you have an existing stereo receiver, you can add a separate surround-sound processor to handle extra speakers. Speakers must be carefully selected and positioned for best sound. What you need will depend on the size and sound-absorbing qualities of your room. For an unobtrusive look, speakers can be recessed into the wall or ceiling.

Televisions are available with a choice of features: direct-view, rear-projection, front-projection, flat-screen, and high-definition. Ask for some showroom help in unraveling your options. Just as important are compatible cable and wiring connections. If you choose to install your own home theater system, see Sunset's *Complete Home Wiring* book for details on components, placement, and wiring.

This seamless makeover from garage to cozy media room required much attention to detail. Floor coverings, paint, and cabinets were matched to those in the adjoining kitchen, and window size and style were coordinated.

The graceful transition between the remodeled kitchen/family room and a wide deck creates a feeling of spaciousness. Transom windows above the French doors brighten the kitchen's once-gloomy high ceilings.

Need help?

Depending on the scope of the job and your time and abilities, you may want to call on professional assistance. Finding the right help need not be daunting. Look for someone who is technically and artistically skilled, has a proven track record, and is adequately insured against any mishaps on the job. It is also important to work with someone with whom you and your family feel comfortable. A remodel is more than just a construction project; it's a personal matter.

ARCHITECTS. Architects are state-licensed professionals with degrees in architecture. Many are members of the American Institute of Architects (AIA). Trained to create designs that are structurally sound, functional, and aesthetically pleasing, they also know construction materials, can negotiate bids from contractors, and can supervise the actual work. If structural calculations must be made, architects can make them; other professionals need state-licensed engineers to design structures and sign working drawings. If your remodel involves major structural changes, an architect should definitely be consulted.

INTERIOR DESIGNERS. Even if you are working with an architect, you may wish to call on an interior designer for the finishing touches. A designer's services can be as simple as editing and arranging what you already have or as complex as creating a complete redesign. Designers can offer fresh, innovative ideas and advice, including updates on the increasingly sophisticated field of lighting design. Many belong to the American Society of Interior Designers (ASID).

GENERAL CONTRACTORS. Contractors specialize in construction, although some have design skills as well. General contractors may do all the work themselves, or they may hire qualified subcontractors, order construction materials, and see that the job is completed to contract. Contractors can also secure building permits and arrange for inspections.

SUBCONTRACTORS. If you act as your own contractor, you will have to hire and supervise subcontractors for specialized jobs such as wiring, plumbing, and tiling. You'll be responsible for permits, insurance, and possibly even payroll taxes.

making your plans

MEASURING ALL OF THE PERIMETERS *and elements of the area you plan to renovate will increase your awareness of the existing space. Scale drawings serve as a good foundation for design and also may satisfy your local building department's permit requirements. If you decide to consult a professional about your project, you may save money by providing measurements and drawings.*

Drawing your plan

Use your drawings to bring your ideas to life, to check fit, to experiment, and to revise and revise and revise. Good plans, drawn to scale on paper, will save much labor down the road and will ensure the most efficient use of materials.

ARCHITECTURAL SYMBOLS

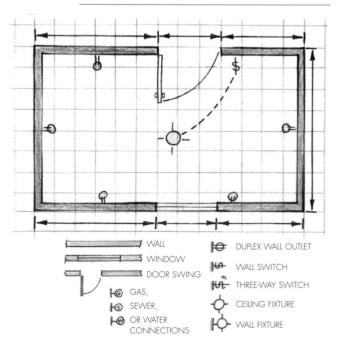

▭ WALL	⊖ DUPLEX WALL OUTLET
▭ WINDOW	⊖ WALL SWITCH
▱ DOOR SWING	⊖ THREE-WAY SWITCH
⊖ GAS,	⊘ CEILING FIXTURE
⊖ SEWER,	⊖ WALL FIXTURE
⊖ OR WATER CONNECTIONS	

Several computer software programs can help you create floor plans with elevations easily and quickly. Computer-aided design (CAD) software shows you how a room looks in three dimensions and allows you to move walls and windows and drag furniture and fixtures in and out at will. Or you can purchase design and layout kits that contain graph paper and scaled-to-size appliance and cabinet templates.

Take all measurements accurately, since even a fraction of an inch counts in fitting together the elements of a layout. To record your measurements, draw a rough sketch of the perimeter (including doors, windows, recesses, and projections) and any relevant adjacent areas. Don't worry about scale at this point, but make your sketch large enough to write all dimensions directly on it, exact to ⅛ inch.

Making it fit

A floor plan drawn to scale gives you a bird's-eye view of how your space is laid out. For neat, readable floor plans, start by attaching graph paper (four squares per inch) to a smooth surface with masking tape. Use a ruler or T-square to

Stone walls, beamed ceiling, and antique maple chopping block add warmth and character to a design that also easily incorporates the latest high-tech appliances.

draw horizontal lines with a pencil, a triangle to draw vertical lines, and a template or compass to show which way each door swings.

Using a scale of ¼"or ½"= 1' (or whatever is convenient for you), map the outer dimensions of the room, noting doors (and their direction of swing), windows, and any fixed architectural features, such as built-in bookcases or a fireplace. Be accurate in converting your measurements to scale.

Indicate the placement of outlets, light fixtures, wall switches, heaters, and vents. Note window dimensions and height from the floor, plus the measurements of any door frames, window trim, and baseboards that might affect furniture placement, window treatments, or wall coverings.

To identify the various elements in your floor plan, use the architectural symbols shown under the basic floor plan on the facing page.

Vaulted to 14 feet, this glass-walled 20- by 20-foot addition opens a once-small seating area off the kitchen to views of an azalea garden and a wooded hillside.

spatial illusions

NO ONE KNOWS WHY, *but when you enter a room that is 1.618 times longer than it is wide, that space appears harmonious and inviting. This was the formula used by the Greeks when they created the Parthenon. But don't despair if your space doesn't match these ideal dimensions. Various strategies can make an area appear larger or smaller.*

A matter of dimension

Because a floor plan encourages us to think in terms of only two dimensions, many people feel a layout is complete after they have measured the length and width of a space and positioned windows and doors. Not so: the height of the space must also be considered.

We tend to think high ceilings make spaces appear bigger than low ceilings do, but a visual perception may work against that theory. If the distance to the ceiling is the largest dimension, our attention is naturally drawn upward to marvel at the height instead of appreciating what the space offers at eye level. If length and width are greater than height, that is where our attention is focused, and the room feels more spacious.

A room's height needs to be compatible with its length and width. A 10-foot ceiling might feel right in a 25-foot-wide great room, but it could

Varied ceiling heights, a low stone wall, and different patterns of Saltillo floor tiles create distinct living and dining areas and direct the flow of traffic.

Color helps define a well-organized multipurpose space. Sunny yellow walls give the kitchen and breakfast area (left) a warm glow, while a comfortable blue sofa beckons from the sitting area (below).

make a smaller space resemble an elevator shaft. People need to feel physically comfortable with a room's height, too. If you're tall, a 7-foot ceiling will make you feel like bending your head every time you enter the room.

Enlarging space

Choreographers know that a theater stage "comes alive" when an imaginary diagonal line is used to create more dynamic space. It's a simple matter of mathematics: just as the hypotenuse of a triangle is the longest line, the diagonal view in a square room—from corner to corner—is the longest dimension. Create views to direct the eye along this long diagonal—to a window or other focal point—and the space will be perceived as larger than it actually is. An unobstructed sight line also makes the entire room appear more welcoming, inviting people in and making a gathering space seem more usable than a tucked-away living room does.

Maximizing the view of a patio or garden with windows or glass doors blurs the lines between the interior and exterior of the house, giving a room a feeling of additional space.

Hanging a mirror adjacent to a window wall reflects the view and further amplifies space.

Color can be used to trick the eye, too. Light colors reflect light, making a room feel larger. Cool hues, such as blues and greens, are considered "receding," appearing more distant than they really are and making a room feel calm and spacious. A standard approach is to paint walls white, but light-value colors like chamois, fawn, or celadon can be just as space-enhancing.

Texture works like color in influencing a room's sense of space. Using similar textures throughout an area helps unify a design, visually enlarging the space as well as creating a mood.

Place large furnishings against walls to keep from breaking up any open space. Sofas and chairs with open arms and exposed legs will allow light to spill around and under them, creating an airier effect. Because glass-topped tables don't interrupt space, they also make rooms seem larger.

Maximize precious floor space with open vertical storage: floor-to-ceiling bookcases or a tall hutch. Choose modest-size furnishings to create a sense of spaciousness. But to keep a room

from feeling like a dollhouse, include a larger piece or two to visually anchor the space.

Subdividing large spaces

Open floor plans and spacious great rooms are the norm in contemporary home design, but they can lack a cozy, intimate feeling and present certain design challenges. Various strategies can be used to tame the space, subtly carving it up without adding walls.

If you are remodeling or building an extension to your house, your options for defining areas within a gathering place are multiplied. Because uniform ceiling heights lend a homogeneous feel to a space, simply raising or lowering part of a ceiling will add interest and establish distinct activity areas. A dining area becomes more dramatic when the ceiling over the space is lowered. Remodeling also makes it possible to change floor levels between areas. A few steps down will handily divide a seating space from the kitchen and dining areas.

To avoid a "ballroom" effect in your great room, with furniture lined up against the walls, you can create inner "rooms" by dividing the larger confines into activity areas. In the seating area, start by creating a conversation grouping around a prominent focal point, such as a fireplace or other strong architectural element. The backs of the seating can form spatial boundaries. A secondary seating area might consist of two club chairs, a table, and a reading lamp near a built-in bookcase wall.

Arrange furniture compactly to hold subarea seating together. Link different areas of the seating space with common flooring, such as hardwood or carpet; delineate and anchor inner rooms with area rugs. Simply changing the direction of an area rug can redefine the imaginary perimeter of an inner room. Placing a low chest or other piece of furniture between distinct areas not only creates an air of separation without blocking a view, but also adds storage space.

Work out a plan that guides foot traffic around, rather than through, inner rooms. Allow

---

FURNITURE DIMENSIONS

To outfit your room, play around with furniture on the floor plan you have prepared. One initially time-consuming but worthwhile way to do this is to cut out pieces of paper scaled to represent the size and shape of the furniture you will be using. Below are some standard dimensions for basic dining and living room furniture.

	WIDTH	DEPTH
SOFA	78"–90"	34"–38"
LOVE SEAT	60"–70"	34"–38"
CHAIR	28"–36"	28"–36"
ARMLESS CHAIR	22"–28"	22"–28"
COFFEE TABLE (SQUARE)	24"–48"	24"–48"
COFFEE TABLE (RECTANGLE)	24"–48"	16"–28"
COFFEE TABLE (ROUND)	18"–32"	
END TABLE	14"–24"	14"–24"
SOFA TABLE/CONSOLE	48"–72"	15"–20"
DINING TABLE (SQUARE)	36"–48"	26"–48"
DINING TABLE (RECTANGLE)	60"–84"	34"–42"
DINING TABLE (ROUND)	36"–60"	
DROP-LEAF TABLE	36"–72"	21"–63"
DINING CHAIR (ARMS)	22"–24"	16"–24"
DINING CHAIR (ARMLESS)	18"–22"	16"–24"
BUFFET/LOW CABINET	48"–72"	16"–26"

A gentle arch and stock columns visually divide the sitting and dining areas of this gathering room (left). Angling the granite-topped island in the kitchen (below) gained space for the owners and helped divert traffic around the food preparation area.

30 to 36 inches of clearance between major furnishings for easy passage, 18 inches between a coffee table and sofa or between chairs.

Color is another easy way to define different areas. If you can clearly see one part of the great room from another, you'll need to relate their colors. This is a perfect situation for using color complements (hues that work well together) or varying tones of the same color. However, using a constant color for trim—baseboards, cornices, and doors—will give the gathering space a more unified look.

As well as giving people a chance to be together, a gathering space should offer them the chance to be alone, in ones and twos. A small alcove at the edge of any room, created either as an architectural feature or simply by arranging furniture, gives one or two people the opportunity to sit in comfort off by themselves. The set-apart space might have a different style to mark its distinction. In a light and airy gathering place, an alcove can become a sheltering, book-lined alternative. Or a corner of a dark room might be turned into a sunroom, filled with light and flowers.

bringing in light

LIGHT CAN LITERALLY TRANSFIGURE *an area. Welcome daylight into a room by means of carefully placed windows, skylights, a window wall, or glass doors. When planning interior lighting, first consider how people will use the room. Lighting separate areas discretely can divide a room into several activity spaces—without a remodel.*

Ringing the walls with soffits for low-voltage lighting, washing the fireplace with light, and illuminating a built-in display area transformed a once-bland family room.

Blurring boundaries

Consider windows to be see-through walls, a way to extend the inside to the outside. Windows connect us to the outer world and, if carefully positioned, can fill our houses with light and views. Think of a window also as an interior composition, a painting that is part of the wall.

If you want clear views of the outside from a seating area, position windows not more than 2'6" off the floor. Windows higher than that will limit the view; you won't be able to see anything below the horizon line. A window in the middle of a flat surface defines a view in a single direction; a corner window (two windows that meet at the corner of a room) presents no boundaries to the view.

Clerestory windows and frameless windows at the edge of a ceiling make spaces feel bigger because they become part of both the wall and the ceiling. The ceiling is painted with light, making it almost appear to float.

Glass patio doors are unrivaled when it comes to bringing in the outdoors. French doors and

A 20-foot-high ceiling gives this casual gathering place a spacious feeling and brings in additional daylight. Three west-facing windows (above) set into the gable augment a pair of casement windows over the kitchen sink. The high windows were kept small to avoid excess heat gain. The light look is carried throughout the inviting space (left), in furnishings as well as surface materials. Varied textures enliven the room's soothing neutral color scheme.

This study's low-voltage lighting was designed to look "soft," in contrast to the hard, industrial appearance of concrete and stone. Light grazing the stone wall provides ambient fill; it's created by a string of reflector lamps hidden inside a light well.

sliding patio doors are the traditional choices for bridging exterior and interior living spaces. Both types double as windows, offering views, light, and ventilation.

Interior doors can affect the light in a room, too. Glazed panels, bifolds, pockets, French doors, and Japanese shoji panels all let light pass from space to space. You can close off a home office or media room from the rest of a gathering space for privacy or energy efficiency, then open it up when sunny weather—or mood—dictates. Bifolds, pockets, shoji panels, and folding doors succeed when there is no space for a swinging door; accordion, or folding, doors can temporarily close off one area from another.

Artificial light

Light is the primary tool at your disposal for changing the mood of a room, making a single area perform double duty. Use bright lighting in an eating area, and the space is illuminated for

family dining; subdue the lighting to turn this dining area into an elegant place to entertain.

Light can also be used to differentiate one part of a room from another. By lighting different areas with different intensities, you can distinguish spaces within the larger room.

Designers separate artificial lighting into five categories: ambient, task, accent, portable, and kinetic.

AMBIENT, or general, lighting creates a bright, pleasant level of illumination—enough, say, for watching television or navigating safely through a room. Incandescent lighting is the preferred choice because of its warm, flattering tone. Ceiling-mounted fixtures usually are used to provide diffuse illumination.

TASK lighting floods a specific area where a visual activity, such as reading or sewing, takes place. This is often achieved with individual glare-free fixtures directed onto work surfaces, such as under-cabinet lights. Ceiling-mounted

The lighting plan in this family-friendly room is simple, in keeping with the home's classic Georgian style. The chandelier offers ambient light, portable lamps provide task lighting, and the fireplace adds a kinetic glow.

lights can also be used for task lighting over kitchen islands.

ACCENT lighting, primarily decorative, is often used to highlight architectural and design elements, set a mood, and provide drama. Like task lighting, it consists largely of directional light. Wall-washing is a broad, evenly dispersed form of accent lighting that can add drama to an entire wall. Use it to show off an architectural feature, an art collection, or another distinctive part of your room.

PORTABLE lighting provides dramatic accents throughout the room. Examples include table lamps, picture lights, and uplighting for plants. This easy-to-add form of lighting is a great way to evoke mood without the expense of recessed installations.

KINETIC lighting is a moving force—flickering, leaping, darting—that is used to create an exciting, romantic, or hypnotic atmosphere. Firelight and candlelight are two intriguing forms.

The right light

Dull or dark surfaces absorb light; glossier surfaces reflect it. A white ceiling can reflect as much as 90 percent of all light aimed at it, while dark flooring can absorb 90 percent of the light.

You have several options for toning down too much light: installing diffusers or lowering the wattage of bulbs, repositioning light sources, or making surfaces less reflective. Consider adding darker colors and eliminating highly polished furnishings, such as brass.

To add brightness, on the other hand, you might paint your walls a lighter color or bounce light around the room by means of refractive surfaces like mirrors and crystal chandeliers.

If you have a corner where light doesn't seem to penetrate, you can brighten it with portable lighting. Make sure lampshades are translucent, not opaque. For an evening party, you might add a collection of candles or cone-shaped uplights.

storage solutions

WILLIAM MORRIS, *one of the founders of the Arts and Crafts Movement of furniture design, proclaimed more than a century ago: "Do not keep anything in your house that you do not know to be useful or believe to be beautiful." This is a good organizing principle for storage. In a home redesign, consider every space as a potential storage spot for useful items; plan special places to display beautiful objects.*

Corralling the clutter

In most homes, bits and pieces of daily living are scattered throughout rooms. But getting organized can start with placing storage space where an object is used—from a drawer in a window seat to a broom closet set into a fireplace area.

The best way to create a workable, lasting solution to your organization needs is to introduce the correct storage system. Wall units range from simple, inexpensive shelving to extensive component systems that include cabinets with doors, adjustable shelves, stacks of drawers, and even desks. Whether you choose custom-built units or modular components, these flexible storage systems can help you make space work harder and smarter to control the chaos of clutter.

Many systems can be reconfigured as your needs change—shelves can be raised or lowered, drawers refitted, and cabinets moved from one location to another. Built-ins, for the most part,

This hard-working wall contains niches, bookshelves, storage drawers, and a desk. A television slides out of a cabinet at left and pivots for easy viewing.

are tailored precisely to specific locations in your room and are usually constructed and installed by a woodworking professional.

Individual furniture pieces designed especially for storage, free-standing or custom-fitted, are another option. Furniture has obvious advantages—it's movable, you can see exactly what you're getting, and it can be chosen to match your decor precisely. But you may not be able to find the perfect size or piece you want, and you'll need to consider the placement of storage furniture when you plan seating areas.

Matching storage to space

Different activity areas within a great room call for different storage solutions. Where family members congregate to play games, read, do homework, and listen to music, versatile modular wall systems are especially popular. With their adjustable shelving, cabinets, drawers, and television bays, these units can organize the myriad paraphernalia that tends to clutter family living spaces. Such storage units also serve as display settings for the family's prized collectibles and art objects.

In the dining area, a wall unit featuring deep cabinets, drawers, and shelves can hold dishes, glassware, serving pieces, and even tablecloths. Combined with a countertop, such a unit also provides a place for buffet-style serving.

A phone/mail center in a nook between the kitchen and dining area or an alcove off the living area might serve as a kind of command post for the house, hiding the controls for temperature, air quality, and lighting. Here, too, could be space to put up the family calendar and bulletin board and to store phone books and address books.

New cabinets along one wall of the dining area (above right) double the kitchen's counter space and offer a place to display some handsome collectibles. The rear wall of this family room (right) contains a built-in media center, book and display shelves, and storage cabinets.

GREAT GATHERING PLACES

FOR SHEER INSPIRATION, there's nothing like a showcase home tour to see how other people design interior spaces to match today's lifestyles. The following gallery of innovative fusion rooms is just that. The first two sections demonstrate how different activity areas can be connected for maximum efficiency and aesthetic appeal. Subsequent sections present ways of handling special situations: home offices and other private places, entertainment areas, and rooms planned to take advantage of views. The final part of your gallery tour is reserved for some particularly successful room designs with lasting appeal. STUDY THESE PAGES for ideas to use in your own home. Don't let room sizes or decor deter you from noticing how cleverly space has been used. Whether your own project is large or small, you'll pick up some good design ideas.

kitchen connections

Many great rooms and family rooms revolve around the kitchen, the place where everyone seems to end up eventually. It's the center of a home, the spot where we gather for morning coffee, pay our bills, make phone calls, check children's homework, and talk over the day's events. Guests naturally congregate here to chat with the cook.

Modern home design reflects the importance of this truly multipurpose room, making it the fastest-growing room in the house in terms of space. Kitchens are being designed with more room than ever before for food preparation, eating, and storage. They include space for the new appliances and amenities we desire, from built-in espresso machines to meal-planning centers.

Opening the kitchen area to the living area of your home—or redesigning the kitchen as a gathering room by adding dining and seating space—almost always means knocking out a wall or two. You may want to add an island to divert traffic, provide extra seating and counter space, and hide messy pots and pans from view. Keep in mind that when your kitchen is on display from other parts of an open room, it will need to match the style of the rest of the space. Fortunately, kitchen manufacturers produce cabinets that resemble furniture and surfacing materials that blend with all design styles, from high-tech contemporary to comfortable country. You'll see examples of fresh approaches on these pages.

Pillars replace walls in this light and airy great room. Rugs anchor furniture on the honey maple wood floor and help define seating and dining spaces. The circular glass coffee table mirrors the dining table and reflects the glass cabinet doors. Even the kitchen backsplash (photo at left) is made of glass tiles. Cool colors throughout contribute to a serene and spacious look.

A spinning wheel lends country charm to this inviting family room. Built-in shelving surrounds the windows, offering ample space for books, collectibles, plants, and a television.

A well-planned lighting scheme gives the kitchen a warm glow. Under-cabinet track lights make it easy to reach for hanging utensils; hood downlights keep spices on display. The open dining area (below) lets guests enjoy the fire in the family room.

Both the bank of kitchen cabinets and the cooktop hood echo the gleam of the family room's handsome hardwood floor. Upholstered stools front an island divider, giving some guests places to sit and chat with the chef while others sink into the casual living area's comfy furniture.

A low sectional couch and fold-up blinds assure that the cozy living area (above) receives unobstructed natural light and views of the patio beyond. Resting on an area rug, furniture is arranged for easy television viewing. Recessed lights in the built-in wall unit show off favorite art objects.

When not serving as seating for the dining table, a padded window seat makes an ideal spot for writing letters, paying bills, planning menus, phoning friends, or simply curling up with a good book. Shelves fitted neatly into the alcove keep papers and books organized.

Light and space first attract the eye in the kitchen and dining area of this multilevel contemporary. But it's the carefully crafted design elements that make it so special—a curved kitchen island capped with concrete and stained to resemble faded leather, custom cabinetry finished like furniture, and stained concrete-block flooring with aluminum strips replacing traditional grout. High overhead, fanciful halogen fixtures direct light over cooking and dining areas.

In the soaring living room (above), flooring changes to Douglas fir, stained to match the concrete of the kitchen level. Removable backs and arms allow sofas to be separated into chairs or made into a sectional. Along with sleek metal side chairs, they are placed for viewing the side-by-side fireplace and television (left). Wheels make it easy to roll the glass coffee table out of the way.

Making a bold architectural statement, this kitchen's custom-crafted, four-sided island is truly a center of attention. Layered with colors and then stained red, cabinets were washed to reveal undertones. In a light-filled bay off the kitchen, the dining area gains fine views without being visually separate from the rest of the great room.

Tumbled marble countertops (left) complement the glazed porcelain floor tiles that extend throughout much of the house. Beyond a sweeping arch is the seating area (below), where attention focuses on a stone fireplace with handcrafted mantel. The television hides discreetly behind the doors of the corner armoire.

Graceful arches replace walls to open up a farm-style kitchen to the sitting room and dining room. Dark wood flooring ties the entire space together, while area rugs help create distinct sitting and dining zones.

In the dining area, a curved raised fireplace lends a romantic touch to an evening meal, while a chandelier supplies soft light. With cabinetry designed to resemble freestanding furniture, the kitchen (below) also features granite-topped counters, tiled backsplashes, and the latest appliances.

In an alcove just off the cooking area, a computer looks right at home in the contemporary setting it shares with the dining table and a window seat. All benefit from plenty of natural light. The home office doubles as a center for planning family activities.

From the glass-topped dining table, your view is directed toward the seating area, where an intricately crafted entertainment unit serves as a focal point. Through the doorway beyond, bookshelves line a library that can be closed off for privacy.

One wall of the conversation area (also shown at top on facing page) features a fireplace and artwork illuminated by wall sconces. From the sofa, guests can watch meal preparations, while others may prefer to step through the French doors onto the patio. The console table behind the sofa acts as both room divider and lamp table.

When television and general conversation pall, two comfortable chairs (left) invite people to put up their feet and indulge in a little private talk or peaceful contemplation in a Zen-inspired setting. Glass panels offer framed views of the landscape outside.

great gathering places

modern math

FINDING SPACE for a multifunctional room without adding on to your home calls for creative thinking. But if you study how your existing rooms are currently being used, you may find that space is hiding just a wall away. Is your formal living room open only for guests, while the family crowds around a kitchen table? Removing the walls that separate the living room from the kitchen or dining area could give you a more usable, family-friendly space. Or perhaps there's a laundry room, back porch, or mud room that you can open up as a dining or seating area off the kitchen. A terrace or porch would extend living space if transformed into a sunroom with places for plants and people.

Areas not originally designed as living spaces often present attractive opportunities for expansion. As photos on the following pages show, attached garages are popular choices for converting into family rooms. An attic may offer space for a combination home office and media center. With good lighting, climate control, and the right equipment, you can turn a basement into a recreation room.

As its name implies, a great room accommodates a range of activities. With careful planning, you may be able to divide an existing room into separate activity areas simply by making minor changes. For example, low bookcases can be positioned as room dividers, and cushions can be fitted on a fireplace hearth to create a secondary seating area—without adding an inch of floor space.

An exterior wall once rose where a handsome wood divider now stands, and the former garage has been beautifully transformed. A brick walkway between house and garage was integrated into the new decorating scheme. A custom-designed double couch (photo at left) lets people choose between television and conversation.

The furnishings in this comfortably welcoming gathering space were placed for maximum exposure to the fireplace, a built-in media center, and the view outdoors. The peaked ceiling and artfully bare windows are strong architectural elements; access to the backyard is through the French doors at right. On the other side of the room (below), a large archway was carved through an exterior wall to create a similarly light-filled dining room.

When all elements of a great room are open to view, dividing the space into separate activity areas requires thoughtful planning. The long great room pictured above and at lower right is an example of how it can be done. Though the hardwood flooring was left bare in the kitchen and dining area, a rug was added to define the conversational grouping. Some of the large pieces of furniture were positioned perpendicular to the walls to break up the linear look.

A fish-filled focal point, this handsome aquarium
subdivides a great room into dining and seating areas
without blocking the view. The cabinet on which the tank
rests also provides storage space.

*With a little creativity,
even a small space can
be transformed into
an open plan. Here,
arched openings in
partial walls link the
kitchen with an
intimate seating space
(right) and a dining
area (below), which
doubles as an
extension of the
conversation grouping.
The padded bench in
front of the fireplace
adds seating yet is not
a visual barrier. The
deft choices of fabric
color and patterns
and the modest scale
of the furniture
serve to unify and
enhance space.*

Providing space for everything from artwork and well-read
classics to audio and visual units, the generous bookcases are,
surprisingly, not attached to the wall. Decorative molding was
added to the movable shelves to give them a look of perma-
nence. The floral ottoman acts as both footstool and coffee table.

*"Stretching" interior
space visually by
linking it with a patio
or deck is a favorite
remodeling strategy.
Flanking this
handsome fireplace,
matching sets of
windows above a
pair of window
seats add light and
garden views.*

When both spouses enjoy cooking and entertaining, there's a definite incentive to remodel. This family annexed space on both sides of their existing kitchen and added another 10 feet at the back of the house to create a spacious gathering place. The one-of-a-kind chandelier (lower photo) was made from collected silverware; recessed lighting, on rheostats, gives balanced illumination. Carrying out the cutlery motif, spoon and fork door pulls accent painted floor-to-ceiling cabinets. Open shelving holds cookbooks, magazines, and recipe files.

Finding extra space can be as simple as looking up; at least that was the case for the family who turned their 1913 attic into a combination office (above) and media room (right). As a bonus, they discovered that the original walls and ceiling, though blackened with age, were fitted with fir; all it took was a little soap, water, and oil to restore them to their original good looks.

great gathering places

Adding a media center to your exercise area might be just the motivation you need for more frequent workouts. "Sink-into-them" chairs in the room below are slipcovered with ultra-suede fabric, which can be cleaned easily.

great gathering places

public and private places

ISLANDS ARE POPULAR vacation destinations because they provide a sense of isolation, an escape from the busy world. The same type of retreat is equally important in a home. Where rooms flow into each other with few, if any, interior walls, we need private spaces that are acoustically or visually separate from the open areas.

Such a quiet retreat might be a book-lined getaway for solitary reading or conversation with one or two friends, or it might be a space equipped with desk and computer where family members can work or study. Add movie, television, or stereo equipment and you can transform this private place into a home entertainment center whenever you wish.

It's surprising how little space an "away room" requires. But if there's just no space for a completely separate private place in your layout, you can still carve out an effective retreat within a great room by arranging furniture to create a small seating area apart from the main conversational grouping. And when your only option for a home office is to incorporate it into a living area, you can use a folding screen to block visual distraction. Carpeting will help muffle noise, or a tall bookcase can be positioned to help deflect sound. Minimize the visual impact of home office equipment by blending it into a wall of cabinets, preferably with doors that can be closed to hide the clutter. These pages showcase some family hideaways.

Life is not all work, a fact that the owner of this paneled, well-appointed "away space" realizes. Serious business may be conducted from the corner office (right), but in the sitting area (photo at left) a laptop may be no competition for enjoying a movie or football game with friends.

When a setting calls for warmth, red reigns. Bold and
brazen, the great room above pulsates with energy and
excitement. In contrast, the more intimate seating area up the
brick stairs (right), although tied to the larger space by the
fabric of the window treatment, projects a quieter mood.

*Interior doors can help connect rooms as well as seal them
off; these elegant French doors link a seating area with an
adjacent retreat. The spacious library and home office
invites people to leaf through a book or just enjoy a few
quiet moments. Glass door panels and transom bring
light into both rooms.*

With soaring ceilings and no interior walls, open plans for contemporary houses often forgo getaway rooms; the modern showpiece pictured on these pages is a happy exception. On the upper level, owners share their large work space (above) with a media room. From the curved balcony, they have a bird's-eye view of the seating area below. The dining area, set apart from the rest of the gathering space with columns and a low wall as well as a two-step rise, is given a more compact feel by the scalloped lowered ceiling.

Just off the kitchen and dining area, the home office in the photo at left can be closed off for total privacy, but its wide doorway keeps the space well connected at other times. Chairs at the kitchen island (below left) add seating space for an intimate living area. Notice how the fireplace mantel extends to crown the room divider, which also holds the television.

Wisely, the workspace in this den is oriented so that anyone seated here receives abundant light without glare from the windows. To keep wandering eyes from the distracting view outside, a wall of photographs provides a place to focus inside.

The lower level of this home was transformed into a multipurpose room that accommodates adults and children, family and friends. It's a great place for a few people to get together for coffee and heart-to-heart talks, for kids to hang out with pals, or for an entire family to gather for a holiday meal. With a pull-out sofa near the dining table, the entire level can become spacious private quarters for houseguests.

Well-planned activity areas have furniture positioned so that several pastimes can take place at once. The couch and chairs (above) offer front-row seating for the latest show. Shelves and cabinets can store books, videos, games, and extra bedding for guests. Completely equipped and color-coordinated, the compact kitchen (left) stands ready to serve drinks, snacks, or even meals.

great gathering places

that's entertainment

WHETHER YOU CALL it a great room, a family room, or a media room, the space in which family and friends gather informally tends to be oriented toward entertainment and recreation.

In today's home, that one large entertaining and family area often contains a big-screen television, a VCR, and speakers. For Hollywood-style glamour, some rooms even have a movie screen and overhead projector. If a room in your home is to be used primarily to watch television, you might as well acknowledge that fact and come up with a way to accommodate this ever-bigger-and-better electronic toy in a manner that's flexible, functional, and attractive, too. Often televisions are placed as afterthoughts when, in reality, they may be the room's main feature. If space is limited, a corner wall unit for video and audio equipment can visually anchor it, gearing the area for both entertainment and conversation. While seating must face a screen for best viewing, chairs should be positioned so that family and friends also can comfortably listen to music, play games, or chat.

Games are popular at any age, so pool tables, chess sets, and card tables—and perhaps electronic games as well—are likely to be a high priority. And many families want space for their small children to play with friends (real or stuffed), create magic shows, and build castles of their own. The children-only layout on page 80 may make you wish you were a kid again.

This ornately appointed media room, open to the kitchen and dining nook, is designed for entertaining. From the handsome bar to the damask-covered sofa, the room makes a grand setting in which to enjoy music and conversation over cocktails or to watch an event on the wide-screen television (photo at left).

Elegant yet relaxed, this airy space adapts equally well to family life and to entertaining. Comfortable leather sofas and a variety of woods and textures lend casual appeal. For support when the television is being worked on, a sturdy wood bench (right) was built to fit.

Recessed into a wall of custom cabinets, the wide-screen television can be seen easily from each sofa, but it shares star billing with a fireplace and a cherished painting on another wall. The room's clean contemporary decor is an effective foil for treasures from around the world.

At one end of a rustic-style retreat (left), a billiards table invites a game. In the center of the room, furniture has been pulled away from the walls and allowed to "float" before the hearth of the massive stone fireplace, focal point for the great room. The dining table at the other end of the room (out of view) also receives the flicker of flames.

The epitome of an electronic entertaining center, this media room boasts screen, projector, and surround-sound equipment. Movie-goers here are cushioned in comfort—with their feet up. The projector is suspended unobtrusively from the ceiling, and stereo equipment is concealed in a closet.

Knocking out walls maximized gathering space and enhanced the overall flow of the light-filled conversational setting above and at right. Chairs are on casters for easy rearrangement. Changes in ceiling levels add architectural interest and intimacy.

Tucked into a corner of the great room, a library doubles as a retreat for playing cards or board games. The brass game table has a brushed nickel finish and a vinyl top, with the look and feel of leather without the price. The seats of the rattan chairs are faux leopard skin. French doors extend this quiet corner into the outdoors on fine days.

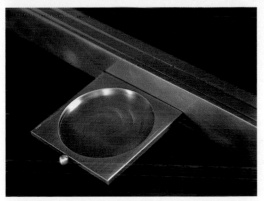

For the height of convenience, individual trays (left) at each corner of the game table slide out to hold drinks.

One section of a
colorful multiuse
cabinet folds down to
form a desk (right),
handy for schoolwork,
a board game, or even
a spread of snacks.
On one side, doors
swing open to reveal
a bar; on the other
side, a television
cabinet is built into
the unit (below).

This recreation room lives up to its name. The game table stands ready for players to take their places, and comfortable chairs

offer relaxed seating for readers, music lovers, and television fans. When closed, the graphically designed wall unit gives little

hint of what lies behind its colorful facade; only books, videos, and audio equipment share its open shelves.

*Under a fabric-draped "big top," the circus has come
to town! Hand-painted clowns and jugglers adorn the walls
of a color-filled kids' retreat (right), while a tightrope
walker balances precariously over a wall sconce (below).
Even a theater awaits an audience. In this sunny space,
all the props are ready for the show to start.*

*An upholstered throne
stands ready for
royalty. Behind the
seat of power, the duck
has all the balls in the
air, but the hang
glider's chute appears
to have been snagged
on the "tent pole."*

great gathering places

rooms with views

HOMES WITH enviable locations have long been built to be oriented toward their best views. But it took architecture's Modern Movement to call to our attention the idea of bringing the landscape indoors through window walls and glass doors. Whether your great room looks out on a sunny deck or a range of mountains, nothing will stretch its space more or provide greater visual satisfaction than placing the outdoors on display from within.

According to architect and design theorist Christopher Alexander, a view that is framed—or even limited—is more satisfying than an unframed panorama. Grouping windows also creates constant light changes and subtle shadow patterns inside, giving a room an elusive appeal. In multilevel homes, like some of those shown in this section, windows not only permit light to flow throughout the house but offer even more expansive views of the ever-changing landscape.

Whether it's better to dress a window or leave it bare depends on the type of window, its location, and the view it frames. If the view is the star, undressed windows may be the best choice. You'll notice that the families represented on the following pages preferred to forgo window treatments as visual barriers, feeling that their sites offered sufficient privacy and sun control. What your window will wear may depend on how your house is situated on your property and how close it is to the neighbors.

Grand in scale and site, the great room pictured at left takes full advantage of its location, offering long-range views from dining-area windows and a more personal look at patio and pool (right) from the conversation space. Extending the pavers blurs the distinction between interior and exterior.

Bathed in light, this glass-walled sunroom opens up the living area and affords expansive hillside views. A contemporary interpretation of a Victorian solarium, the airy, informal space uses brick flooring, rattan furniture, container plants, and floral art to carry out a garden room decor.

With its beautiful wood flooring, informal furnishings, and palette of country-side colors, this great room looks perfectly at ease in its vineyard setting. A combination of fixed windows and French doors offers nonstop views and access to the veranda; the overhang provides shade, eliminating the need for shutters or shades. Recessed lighting brightens the evening scene.

Only the window washer knows for sure where the glass begins and ends in this multi-level hillside home. Decor was kept deceptively spare and light in visual weight to avoid competing with the home's strong structural lines and impressive views.

great gathering places

The view is the focal point at one end of a stylish great room.
From the kitchen island (to right of photo) to the wicker
chairs at left, there are no walls, high furnishings, light
fixtures, or window treatments to spoil the scenic effect. On
the other side of this room (shown on page 32), seating and
dining areas focus on a handsome entertainment unit and
a stone fireplace wall.

Windows often act like
picture frames, offering
tantalizing glimpses of
the landscape without
revealing its entirety.
The muntins on these
windows multiply
the effect, enhancing the
sense of enclosure in
the cozy sitting area
while showcasing
the view.

Under a dramatic angular wood ceiling, the seating area at right is the center of attention inside this ultramodern multilevel. A Bokara rug grounds furnishings in front of the fireplace; a collection of colorful glass, displayed on recessed shelving, adds another focal point. When work calls, a shelf-lined retreat on an upper level houses a home office (bottom photo) open to the gathering space below. Railings throughout the house are standard 4-inch "hogwire" fencing with a powder coat.

From the raised dining area and the music corner (above), walls of windows offer inspiring valley views. Glass doors from the dining level (and the seating area, facing page) lead out to a hillside deck. Flooring in the dining area is stained concrete tiles with a design imprint, The exposed wood beams (left) that support the house make an important design statement.

great gathering places

Opening up the dining, seating, and recreation areas of the rustic-style great room at right, a battery of different window shapes and sizes highlight a 180-degree coastal view. For even more expansive vistas, French doors lead onto a deck.

"Dramatic" and "grand" are terms that leap to mind for the scene from the windows below—and for the interior space as well. If desired, light pours into the room during the day, or blinds can be lowered to moderate its intensity. In the evening, soft recessed ceiling lighting adds intimacy.

All the public spaces of this home are oriented to the scenery outside. Guests who perch on stools in front of the kitchen island (left) get the same grand outlook as those seated in the living and dining areas (above).

lasting impressions

We all have ideas about what makes up the perfect space and how we would like our family to live. The list grows every time we visit a showcase house or run into another problem with our own home's layout. Is the kitchen so poorly laid out that the designated cook has to labor away in solitude? How long has it been since we have eaten dinner around a table? Where can a quiet conversation with a friend be carried on while the children are watching television? Where can we find space for a home office?

We all need gathering places for our family and friends, and as a counterpoint we need private spaces for relaxation, exercise, or homework. To see how some families have achieved a balance, take a look at the following collection of beautifully designed and decorated rooms. Decors differ dramatically, as do room sizes and styles. But all these rooms are alike in the thoughtful planning and the attention to detail that went into creating them.

Combination cooking-dining-living spaces are what today's families frequently choose to reflect their lifestyles. These are often the rooms that best display their owners' personalities. Entertainment areas and private spaces provide clues as to family interests, too. We invite you to take a peek at the rooms on the next several pages for glimpses of how some families live. Your sense of space and style may differ dramatically from these examples, but they should offer inspiration and ideas that you can use.

When space is at a premium, it takes careful planning to arrive at the best design. Placing an entertainment armoire (right) in the corner between two windows and topping it with plants and accessories fills in what could be a "problem" area. Striped and floral fabrics lend a garden feel (photo at left).

Walk right in and sit down—that's the message you get from the comfortable and casual gathering place pictured below. The seating area, located off the kitchen (out of view to the left), offers a pair of roomy chairs and a spacious sectional sofa for taking it easy in front of the hearth. Only a boat model, a telescope, and a long window seat hint at the special appeal of the outside view.

Arches, columns, walls of glass, and a dramatic beamed ceiling—these architectural details tie together and add interest to the meal-planning, dining, and seating areas of the great room shown above and at right. The conversational grouping is arranged to ensure front-row seating for entertainment or cozying up to the fire. Audio-visual equipment hides behind the storage unit's closed doors.

At first glance, the dining area on the facing page, with its gilded chandelier and imposing painting, might make you think you're in a European country manor house. But as you walk through the great room (above), you'll soon notice just how comfortable the elegant setting feels; though formal, the decor exudes warmth, inviting you to pull up a chair to the kitchen island divider and join the party. The diagonal placement of the rug in the conversational grouping adds depth to the room.

A fruit-gathering cherub, ornate molding, and a colorful swag (left) set the decorating theme for this Provençal-inspired kitchen. Learning how to drape and gather swags takes time; "swag holders" that secure fabric at the top of the window will help.

The spare elegance of
well-edited space
imparts a feeling of
sophisticated serenity to
this generously scaled
gathering place. Only
a natural woven mat
connects dining and
seating areas. High
fixed windows flanking
the fireplace bring in
light while preserving
streetside privacy.

From the low table and chairs, diners view the home's inner
courtyard in rectangular sections. By day, the artfully bare
window wall takes an architectural stand; by night, the
courtyard gains added appeal through the use of carefully
positioned exterior lights.

Mahogany gives a rich look to the coffered ceiling and
paneled walls of this great room's entertainment zone.
Seating is directed toward the stone-clad fireplace and a bar
fitted into the corner. Impressive French doors admit light
and permit access to the patio and pool beyond.

Past the railing, through the arch, and up two steps lie the kitchen and eating areas (above). Though the stone tile flooring matches the fireplace facade (facing page), lighter colors and patterned wallpaper help set these spaces apart. In the seating area, blinds were added to an arched window (left) to control sun and prevent glare on the television screen, hidden behind cabinet doors.

It's the fine touches that define a room's character and attract us to the space. Here, decorative molding and trim emphasize windows and doors (above); a well-crafted stairway (right) invites ascent.

Think quality when you consider the beautiful detailing in this Mission-style great room. The polished wood couch, chairs, and coffee table, drawn into an intimate grouping, echo gleaming wood floors. The chandelier over the dining table and the lights hanging above the kitchen island are Arts and Crafts–inspired. Recessed cabinets flanking the windows and a storage unit underneath are among the room's useful and decorative built-ins.

DESIGN ELEMENTS

Comfort, convenience, and CHARM — these are the goals of creating a gathering space that warmly welcomes family and friends. But where do you start? To keep things simple, we focus first on your room's envelope: the walls, ceiling, and floor. Then we let in light with windows, skylights, and doors. ARMED WITH THE BASICS, it's easier to progress to such fine points as layering color, planning artificial lighting, selecting hard-working furnishings, and bringing in the personal touches that express your individuality. Consider your choices from both practical and aesthetic viewpoints, using this chapter as a resource.

Wall Finishes

BOLD, BEAUTIFUL BACKDROPS

Walls and ceiling account for most of your room's square footage, offering large, often blank canvases on which to make an artistic statement about how you live and how you perceive your space. Your wall and ceiling treatments can hide problems, enhance strong points, and pull together a design scheme better than any other element.

Assess your room's basics before making decisions on wall treatment. Start with the quality of light (both natural and artificial), the proportions of the room, and architectural features you may want to downplay or highlight. Soaring ceilings can be "lowered" by painting them a deep, warm color, low ceilings "raised" with a color much lighter than that on the walls. If a room is small and dark, light colors lend a spacious, airy quality. Or the same space can be enlivened with warm, rich colors and textures to give it a cozy feel.

Paint

Paint is what everybody thinks of first when considering the numerous options for wall treatments. Even with paint, your choices are myriad, from a neutral palette to quiet colors or strong ones. Many paint shops and home improvement centers now offer designer-chosen

A dramatic color treatment for an attractive fireplace plays up its architectural style, drawing the eye away from less interesting elements.

palettes that allow you to mix wall, ceiling, and trim colors from room to room with confidence. The hand-sponged and marbleized paint effects that were popular in recent decades have given way to quieter decorative applications, such as combing and color washing, that add depth and texture without calling undue attention to themselves. Some designer paints add fibers that transfer denim, suede, flannel, or other feel-good textures directly onto the wall.

Paint finish affects its color and determines its durability. Flat or matte paints absorb the most light, creating an opaque color, and are usually the best choice for ceilings or living areas. Semigloss and gloss finishes reflect a lot of light and can take vigorous scrubbing, making them ideal for trim as well as food preparation areas, but they do highlight any texture or imperfections in walls.

Water-based latex paint is today's preferred choice over alkyd (oil-based) paint. It is nearly odorless, dries in hours rather than days, and cleans up with soap and water. Alkyd paint has excel-

Muted paint colors provide a soft backdrop for a recessed fireplace nook, allowing attention to focus on artistic and architectural elements.

since paneling boards generally have edges specially milled to overlap or interlock. Hardwood boards are most often milled from oak, maple, birch, and mahogany. Common softwoods include cedar, pine, and fir.

Moldings are back in vogue. You'll find basic profiles at lumberyards and home centers. Specialty millwork shops are likely to offer a wider selection and will often custom-match an old favorite. Prefinished pine or hardwood is fine if you want a stained look, but if you plan to paint your molding, medium-density fiberboard (MDF) is less prone to warping and takes paint better.

Also consider architectural accents such as pediments, pilasters, decorative friezes, and ceiling medallions. New pieces are stocked at home improvement centers, vintage originals at architectural salvage yards and specialty stores.

A decorative accent in its own right, free-form shelving can be located almost anywhere on a wall and extend for any length.

lent durability but takes longer to dry, requires a paint-thinner cleanup, and may make you choose to vacate your house until the odor dissipates.

Wallpaper

Textured or patterned wallpaper can add warmth and dimension to a room as well as soften living spaces. Unsurpassed for hiding imperfections and creating detail in a space that lacks it, wallpaper can produce optical illusions suggesting better proportions in rooms that are too long or too boxy, or whose ceilings are too low or too high. Most papers are relatively simple to install.

Traditional styles are available in updated hues, and coverings such as linen look-alikes and grass cloth can add subtle texture while providing a muted backdrop for furnishings. Embossed wall coverings designed to look like stucco, pressed tin, or plaster fresco can impart a sense of history to a contemporary home.

Wall coverings containing or coated with some sort of vinyl will be the sturdiest and easiest to install. But alternatives abound, including silk and other natural fibers that provide a neutral backdrop. Uncoated choices such as

hand-screened papers are gorgeous but may be difficult to hang. The same is true of foils, which can brighten up a dark space, and brown craft paper, at once simple and sophisticated. You will probably want to seek professional help if you decide to use one of these.

Architectural treatments

From the most elaborate crown molding to the simplest baseboard, millwork can lend architectural interest to almost any space. You can even use it as you would furniture arrangements, to divide a large space into smaller areas—with chair rails to define the dining area, for example. When selecting the style and scale of millwork at your lumberyard, consider your home's architecture as well as its proportions. An elaborate cornice molding would enhance a room of grand, classical proportions, yet look out of place in a smaller, low-ceilinged room.

Solid wood paneling—natural, stained, bleached, or painted—provides a warm ambience in country decorating schemes. Wainscoting is traditional, with a chair rail separating the wood paneling below it from the painted or papered wall above. Installing wood paneling is not a difficult undertaking,

Flooring

THE LOWDOWN ON THE GROUND LEVEL

Although it accounts for only 30 percent of the surface space, flooring is the hardest-working design element in a room. It has a significant impact not only on the overall look of the room but on your budget as well. Whatever flooring you select, don't forget to factor in the cost of installation. However, even high-end looks can be achieved within reasonable means. Ceramic tiles, concrete tiles, and even vinyl can now simulate many beautiful stone materials. Old wood floors can be refinished.

The major categories of floor coverings are resilient, including vinyl, linoleum, cork, and rubber; hard flooring, including tile, stone, and concrete; wood, in all manner of finishes and styles; and soft flooring, in the form of carpeting, matting, and area rugs. As you look at the comparison chart on the facing page, keep the following design considerations in mind.

If you will be mixing floor coverings, it's important to harmonize tone, texture, and scale, and to plan how you'll make the transition from one type of flooring to another. A wood floor can be a versatile backdrop for a large area, while an area rug placed over one section may become a dramatic focal point that pulls together the room's palette.

Whereas the dining area can sustain a floor high in aesthetic value, such as mahogany with an inlay border, the kitchen end of your open plan may call for a water-resistant covering, such as

tile. Vinyl is another practical choice in the kitchen because it cleans up readily and is comfortable to stand on for long periods.

Flooring in seating areas may depend on climate, the need for noise control, and environmental sensitivities. Hot climates suggest cool flooring, such as tile pavers; carpets and rugs are better for colder climes. Tightly looped carpeting also muffles sound. But remember that carpets harbor mites and may be treated with products that aggravate allergies or chemical sensitivities. Whatever soft flooring you buy, be sure it is stain resistant.

Laminate floor, with a photograph of wood under resin, is hard to distinguish from wood. At top, slate tiles dressed up with limestone strips and glass mosaics give an outdoor look.

COMPARING FLOORING

Resilient

Advantages. Softer and quieter underfoot than many other surfaces, resilient floors are flexible, moisture and stain resistant, easy to install, and simple to maintain. A seemingly endless variety of colors, textures, patterns, and styles is available. A relatively new choice is plastic laminate, covering a photo of wood with melamine resin.

Sheet vinyl runs up to 12 feet wide; tiles are generally 12 inches square. Vinyl, cork,

CORK

rubber, and leather are all comfortable to walk on. A polyurethane finish may eliminate the need to wax a vinyl floor.

Disadvantages. Resilients are relatively soft, making them vulnerable to dents and tears, but often these can be repaired. Moisture can collect in poorly jointed seams if resilient flooring isn't properly installed.

Cost. As a category, resilient flooring is modestly priced, though you'll pay a premium for custom and imported products.

Hard tile

Advantages. Durable, attractive, and natural—it's hard to beat clay and stone tile. And with today's sealers, tile is virtually impervious to spills, water, and mud. Clay tiles, from terra-cotta to porcelain, come in every color and design imaginable. Stone tiles range from white marble to black granite, with greens, browns, and grays in between. Economical concrete tiles come in many colors and textures, some mimicking marble and limestone.

CONCRETE TILE

Floor tiles run the gamut of sizes; 8- and 12-inch squares are most common.

Disadvantages. Tile can be cold, noisy, and, if glazed, slippery underfoot; anything that falls on it will take a beating. Porous tile will stain and harbor bacteria if not properly sealed. Grout spaces can be tough to keep clean, though mildew-resistant or epoxy grout definitely helps. Most hard flooring is heavy, so the subfloor must be strong enough to support it.

Cost. Prices range from modest to expensive, depending on the material and finish.

Wood

Advantages. A classic hardwood ages beautifully, feels good underfoot, is relatively easy to care for, and can be refinished when needed rather than having to be replaced. Red and white oak are most commonly used, with maple, birch, and other species also available. Softwoods such as fir and pine provide a rustic look but are more likely to dent and scratch. Environmentally sustainable timber like bamboo is now available as an alternative for eco-conscious consumers. Surface treatments—from bleaching to stain-

WOOD STENCIL

ing to painting—can protect wood floors and increase design options.

Disadvantages. Moisture damage and inadequate floor substructure are two bugaboos. Maintenance is another issue; while some surfaces can be mopped or waxed, some cannot. Bleaching and some staining processes may wear unevenly, a difficult problem to correct.

Cost. Depending on wood species, grade, and finish, cost is moderate to high; wood free of knots and of consistent color and grain will be more expensive.

Soft coverings

Advantages. Carpets, matting, and area rugs can disguise damaged flooring, provide warmth and softness underfoot, reduce noise, conserve energy, function as a focal point, and define a room's subareas. Carpeting is available in an array of materials—synthetic fibers (nylon, acrylic, Olefin, rayon), natural fibers (wool, cotton), or a blend. Wool is the most durable, care-free nylon the most popu-

SEA GRASS MATTING

lar. Tightly woven commercial products offer durability and trim appearance.

Disadvantages. Generally, the more elaborate the material and weave, the greater the potential for problems from moisture absorption, staining, and mildew. Area rugs need nonslip pads beneath them to extend their life and protect the floor. Matting, while economical, is not as soft underfoot and may be difficult to clean.

Cost. Price varies considerably, with wool being the most expensive.

Windows

SHEDDING LIGHT ON NEW DESIGNS

Whether you'd like to build a sunroom, add on an old-fashioned bay, or light up a dark corner, you're in luck. Manufacturers, home improvement centers, and window stores showcase literally thousands of window styles, including arched casements and fixed windows in semicircles, ovals, trapezoids, and other shapes, all with a dizzying assortment of framing and glazing options. If the window you want isn't standard, many manufacturers will make one to your specifications.

Window options

If you're switching to a different window style or size, check local building codes before buying; codes specify ventilation requirements and often insist on enough window space for access by firefighters. Also, energy codes govern the allowable ratio of glass to floor area.

Operable windows include double-hung, casement, sliding, and awning types. Which you choose depends partly on your home's style and partly on your ventilation needs. Frames come in wood, clad wood (encased in aluminum or vinyl), aluminum, vinyl, steel, or fiberglass. Generally, aluminum windows are the least expensive, wood and clad wood the most costly. Vinyl- or aluminum-clad wood windows and all-vinyl windows require little maintenance.

Many of the greatest strides in window technology are taking place in glazing. Ordinary flat glass can be strengthened, coated, and tinted to block solar heat yet offer pleasant light inside and a clear view outside. Insulating glass is made of two or more panes of glass sealed together with space between the panes to trap air. Low-emissivity (low-e) glass adds a transparent metallic coating that deflects heat —outward in warm weather, inward in cold weather—and blocks the sun's ultraviolet rays. Low-e glass is nearly as clear as untreated glass. Some manufacturers use argon gas between the panes of insulating glass to increase energy efficiency even more.

Thanks to insulating glass, wintry weather is kept at bay beyond the graceful, arched windows of this cozy sunroom. At top, blackout blinds hidden behind the door valances and the cornice of the arched window above offer the possibility of total darkness.

WINDOW WORDS

Strange, intimidating words seem to orbit the subject of windows. Here's a crash course in standard window jargon, enough to help you brave a showroom or building center.

Apron. An applied interior trim piece that runs beneath the unit, below the sill.

Casement. A window with a frame that hinges on the side, like a door.

Casing. Wooden window trim, especially interior, added by owner or contractor. Head casing runs at the top; side casings flank the unit.

Cladding. A protective sheath of aluminum or vinyl covering a window's exterior wood surfaces.

Flashing. Thin sheets, usually metal, that protect the wall or roof from leaks near the edges of windows or skylights.

Glazing. The window pane itself—glass, acrylic plastic, or other clear or translucent material. It may be one, two, or even three layers thick.

Grille. A decorative, removable grating that makes an expanse of glass look as though it is made up of many smaller panes.

Jamb. The frame that surrounds the sash or glazing. An extension jamb thickens a window to match a thick wall.

Lights. Separately framed panes of glass in a multipane window; each light is held by muntins.

Low emissivity (low-e). Denoting a high-tech surface coating treatment that sharply improves the thermal performance of glass, especially in double-glazed windows, at little added cost.

Mullion. A vertical dividing piece; whereas muntins separate small panes of glass, mullions separate larger expanses of glass or whole windows.

Muntin. A slender strip of wood or metal framing a pane of glass in a multipane window.

R-value. Measure of a material's ability to insulate; the higher the number, the lower your heating or cooling bills should be.

Sash. A window frame surrounding glass. It may be fixed or operable.

Sill. An interior or exterior shelf below a window unit. An interior sill may be called a stool.

U-value. Measure of the energy efficiency of all the materials in the window; the lower the U-value, the less the energy waste.

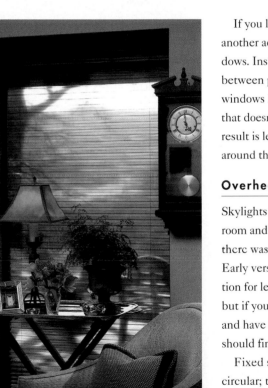

If you live in a cold climate, consider another advancement, warm-edge windows. Instead of an aluminum spacer between panes of insulating glass, these windows have a less conductive spacer that doesn't transfer heat as readily. The result is less buildup of condensation around the edge of the window.

Overhead styles

Skylights can bring light deep into a room and create a sense of drama where there was merely a blank ceiling before. Early versions gained a nagging reputation for leaks, condensation, or heat loss, but if you buy a quality skylight today and have it properly installed, you should find these concerns unfounded.

Fixed skylights vary from square to circular; they may be flat, domed, or pyramidal in profile. Most manufacturers offer several ventilating models.

If there's space between the ceiling and roof, you'll need a light shaft to direct light to the room below. It may be straight, angled, or splayed (wider at the bottom).

Think of roof windows as a cross between windows and skylights. Typically installed on sloping walls, they have sashes that rotate on pivots on two sides, which permits easy cleaning.

Window dressing

If you opt for an architecturally elegant window, a decorative bay or bow, or a picture window framing a magnificent view, you may choose to leave it bare. Otherwise, a variety of coverings can dress up openings that are not architecturally noteworthy or where privacy and light control are paramount concerns. You'll find blinds, shades, and shutters in many colors and finishes.

These translucent shades provide a neutral background for the room's decor while softening the light coming in from outside. The view through to the terrace visually extends the room's dimensions.

Doors

WINDOWS TO WALK THROUGH

One favorite remodeling strategy is to "stretch" interior space by bridging it to the outdoors with a sunny patio or deck. Hinged French doors or sliding doors help link living space and garden while doubling as view walls. Glazed interior doors are also light catchers. Open or closed, they let sunlight pass from room to room; when shut, they seal off noise and drafts.

Patio doors

The typical French door is hinged wood with a large tempered-glass panel (sometimes overlaid with a decorative grille) or smaller glass panes separated by muntins. French doors usually come in pairs, with an inactive door held stationary by slide bolts at the top and bottom and an active door closing and locking against it.

Sliding doors take up less room than French doors. They consist of two-door panels of tempered glass in wood, vinyl, or aluminum frames. A sliding door may be purchased with one large glass panel (with or without grille) or multiple panels with muntins.

Like windows, patio doors come with a variety of glazing options. Because of the expanse of glass, it's critical to choose wisely. Low-e glazing (see page 113) can prevent heat absorption, trap existing heat, and prevent fabrics from fading. Double glazing not only adds energy efficiency but also allows shades or blinds to be installed between the

glass panes. Patio door glazing must be tempered or laminated.

Window showrooms and home centers usually stock wood, clad wood, and vinyl doors as well as traditional aluminum sliding doors. Clad wood is a popular choice, combining the traditional wood feel and look inside with a tough, maintenance-free exterior. Vinyl doors are tight, smooth, and nearly maintenance free and won't swell and contract with changing weather as wood can. Today's aluminum sliding doors, outfitted with energy-efficient glazing, effective weather-stripping,

and thermal breaks, have been greatly improved over earlier models.

Patio doors are available in a variety of widths; 80 inches is the standard height, 6 feet the standard width. When sizing up your choices, you'll need to determine door swing or slide direction (both specified when you are facing the unit from outside), plus wall thickness. Designers and architects love French doors to open outward, though installers feel these models are tougher to weatherproof.

To give patio doors added emphasis, think about ganging transoms above

them or installing matching sidelights or tall casement windows alongside them.

If you live in a mild climate, there's another option: tall, movable door panels that slide on tracks from the ceiling. On sunny days, these panels can open a living space or sunroom to the elements.

Interior doors

Adding glass panels to interior doors keeps them from becoming impenetrable barriers. Glazed interior doors can be found at home centers and door specialty suppliers. You can buy most of them as separates or as kits—with or without the hardware.

For personal space such as an office area, consider fitting doors with privacy locks that have a locking button on the inside but can be easily opened with a key, screwdriver, or paper clip in an emergency.

Other options for dividing interior spaces of a multipurpose room are bifold and pocket doors and track-mounted screens that can be closed for solitude, opened for entertaining—without loss of floor space.

Similar to French doors, two sets of multifold glass-paned doors (facing page) open the great room to a jasmine-wreathed patio. At right, a pocket door and track-mounted sliding screens offer uncluttered solutions to door-clearance problems. Though the pocket door (top) is rectangular, the curved door rail creates the illusion that it is arched. Traditional shoji screens (bottom) function as both interior doors and movable wall sections. For television-viewing privacy, they can just be pulled shut.

Editing with Color

A CHOICE OF PERSONAL PALETTE

As Martha Stewart says, "A house is not a home until it is full of color—it's the inspiration for decorating." Certainly color does more to set the mood and style of a room than any other design element. To help you develop the skill and confidence to create a color scheme from scratch, we unravel color vocabulary and interpret a color ring.

Color talk

Hue is just another name for color. Turquoise and fuchsia are hues; so are softer colors like lilac and sage. Both terms are used in art and design. Three characteristics provide the key to combining colors successfully. **VALUE** means the lightness or darkness of a color. Robin's egg blue is a light value of blue, washed denim a medium value, and navy a dark value. **TEMPERATURE** refers to a color's warmth or coolness. Take a look at the color ring on the facing page. If you draw an imaginary line across it from yellow-green to red-violet, the colors to the left—yellows, oranges, and reds—are warm. These colors tend to make a room feel cozy. Cooler hues—those to the right of your imaginary line—can make a room feel calm and spacious. **INTENSITY** describes a color's brightness. The colors on the color ring are fully intense, or "saturated." Low-intensity colors, on the other hand, are more muted. Lime, for example, is an intense yellow-green, willow a less intense version of the same hue.

Designers consider intensity to be color's great unifier. That is, you can combine any colors if they are similar in intensity; they just seem to belong together. If you take a look at color palette cards from paint manufacturers, you'll see that disparate colors with the same intensity are naturally harmonious. For example, bright red and soft sage might clash, but a less intense brick color would be compatible with the sage.

Color and space

Using color to define or alter space is really about creating illusions. The rule of thumb is that light and cool colors visually expand space, whereas dark and warm colors make it seem smaller. Similarly, low-intensity colors are thought to make a room seem more spacious, intense ones to contract it.

In reality, these optical effects are modified by many factors, such as the

Bright fabrics and table mats and vibrant wall art add rich layers of color, texture, and pattern to a charming great room.

A common color, lemon yellow, is the tie that binds a delightful mix of florals, plaids, and solids in this sunny bay.

quantity and quality of light a room receives. Painting walls a light color will not transform a naturally dark room into an open, airy space. A rich color will not necessarily add intimacy to a large room. Sometimes it's best to go with what you have rather than try to work against it.

But do consider putting color to use when you want to change the apparent proportions of a room. Painting the end wall of a long, narrow room a warmer, darker color than the others can create the illusion of a better-proportioned room. In a square room, painting one wall a more intense color can diminish a boxy look.

Color can also affect our sense of adjoining space. Carrying the same paint color and flooring throughout makes a smooth visual transition, opening up the space. If you prefer distinctly separate areas, on the other hand, use different colors or intensities of color.

USING A COLOR RING

Most of us don't think of consulting a color ring when we choose colors for our homes. The colors shown on the ring appeal to a relatively narrow audience, while the sophisticated nuances of color found in home furnishings—celadon, aubergine, cinnabar—never appear. Yet the pure hues on the color ring are the source of all colors used in decorating.

Most decorator colors also contain some black, white, or gray. But spice, pumpkin, and peach, for example, come from pure orange on the color ring; olive is just a dark yellow-green; and iris is really a light blue-violet.

Once you realize that all hues have a place on the color ring, you can make it work well for planning your decorating scheme.

Primary colors—red, blue, and yellow—are so named because they cannot be created from other colors. Instead, they make up all other colors, in different combinations and proportions. Intense primaries in large quantities can be harsh; lower-intensity versions of these colors—such as cranberry, navy, and gold—are easier to live with.

Secondary colors result from mixing two primaries. Red mixed with yellow makes orange, blue mixed with yellow makes green, and blue mixed with red makes violet.

Intermediate colors are created when a primary color is combined with an adjacent secondary color. For example, red (primary) and violet (secondary) combine to make red-violet. Starting with yellow and moving clockwise around the color ring, the intermediate colors are yellow-green, blue-green, blue-violet, red-violet, red-orange, and yellow-orange. More complex than primary or secondary colors, intermediates are among the most versatile of decorating hues.

The relationship of colors on the ring indicates their affinities and contrasts. Adjacent colors (blue, blue-violet, and violet, for example) are called *analogous*. These three share a common color—in this case, blue. Opposing colors, such as blue and orange, are *complementary* colors, meaning that they balance one another in visual temperature. Colors that are approximately opposite are also well balanced; they're known as *near complements*. Lavender blue (a version of blue-violet) is the near complement of yellow.

Lighting

HIGHLIGHTING THE LATEST FIXTURES

A good lighting design creates the atmosphere you want for your multipurpose room. The most successful designs accomplish this task in an energy-efficient fashion, with careful consideration given to selecting each type of fixture and bulb.

Fixtures

Recessed ceiling lights (ideally placed about 4 to 6 feet apart) are the most popular choice for today's general lighting needs. You can also use the traditional central ceiling fixture or indirect light sources such as uplights, wall fixtures, table lamps, or fluorescent-tube lighting concealed in a cove near the ceiling.

Task lighting to illuminate specific activity areas can come from built-in fixtures (such as an under-cabinet light illuminating a countertop), from track fixtures that offer pinpoint lighting, or from portable, free-standing fixtures that direct light where needed. Low-voltage cable lights combine the flexibility of standard track fixtures with a dash of high-tech style.

Accent lighting is often concealed behind a valance or soffit (strip lighting, rope lighting, or small, plug-in lights) or designed to blend into the background (adjustable track lighting or recessed mono-spotlights). About five times brighter than the general lighting in an area, accent lighting should be posi-

tioned at an angle that minimizes glare on the featured object.

Decorative lighting draws attention to itself. Plan fixtures like chandeliers, table lamps, wall sconces, or hanging pendants as part of the overall lighting scheme, as they can also provide ambient or even task lighting.

Because more than one type of activity takes place in a great room, a range of light sources is needed. Ideally, each should have a separate control (or a dimmer on a master control) so that a variety of lighting levels can be selected, from soft glow to radiant brightness.

Bulbs

As the chart on the facing page illustrates, there are three types of light bulbs: incandescent, fluorescent, and quartz halogen.

INCANDESCENT bulbs are the most familiar in households; they come in dozens of shapes and sizes and provide a flattering, natural-looking light. Low-voltage incandescent lighting is especially useful for accent lighting. Operating on 12 or 24 volts, these lights require transformers (sometimes built into the fixtures) to step down the voltage from 120-volt household circuits. Low-voltage fixtures are relatively expensive to buy but can be energy- and cost-efficient in the long run.

FLUORESCENT tubes are unrivaled for energy efficiency. They use only one-fifth to one-third the electricity of a standard incandescent bulb and

A successful design for a gathering place, like the serene room shown above, incorporates a lighting plan that features energy- and cost-efficient fixtures and bulbs.

Little high-tech fixtures specially designed for halogen bulbs balance artistic form with bright light output.

last 10 to 20 times longer. Even though fluorescents cost more initially, they're the least expensive lights to operate and the most earth-friendly choices available. In some places, general lighting for new kitchens must be fluorescent.

While older fluorescents offered poor color rendition, today's versions are available in a range of color-corrected tubes. A compact fluorescent tube can be substituted for an incandescent bulb in many traditional fixtures and also fits specially designed built-ins and free-standing torchères. Overhead fluorescent fixtures come in a wide range of decor-friendly styles and are lauded for their soft, shadowless general lighting. **HALOGEN** bulbs are incandescents' high-tech, energy-efficient cousins, producing a whiter, brighter light. Halogen bulbs are much smaller, making them great candidates for task and accent lighting and for the tiny, sleek, artistic fixtures being designed today. The popular MR-16 bulb creates the tightest beam; for a longer reach and wider coverage, choose a PAR bulb. These hot-burning bulbs can be used safely only in fixtures designed specifically for them; shop for UL-approved fixtures.

COMPARING LIGHT BULBS AND TUBES

INCANDESCENT

A-bulb
Description. Familiar pear shape; frosted or clear.
Uses. Everyday household use.

T—Tubular
Description. Tube-shaped, from 5" long. Frosted or clear.
Uses. Cabinets, decorative fixtures.

R—Reflector
Description. White or silvered coating directs light out end of funnel-shaped bulb.
Uses. Directional fixtures; focuses light where needed.

PAR—Parabolic aluminized reflector
Description. Similar to auto headlamps; special shape and coating project light and control beam.
Uses. Recessed downlights and track fixtures.

Silvered bowl
Description. A-bulb, with silvered cap to cut glare and produce indirect light.
Uses. Track fixtures and pendants.

Low-voltage strip
Description. Like Christmas tree lights; in strips or tracks, or encased in flexible, waterproof plastic.
Uses. Task lighting and decoration.

FLUORESCENT

Tube
Description. Tube-shaped, 5" to 96" long. Needs special fixture and ballast.
Uses. Shadowless work light; also indirect lighting.

PL—Compact tube
Description. U-shaped with base; 5¼" to 7½" long.
Uses. In recessed downlights; some PL tubes include ballasts to replace A-bulbs.

Compact bulb
Description. Many shapes and sizes, replacing incandescent bulbs without needing special sockets.
Uses. Everyday household use in traditional fixtures.

QUARTZ HALOGEN

High intensity
Description. Small, clear bulb with consistently high light output; used in halogen fixtures only.
Uses. Specialized task lamps, torchères, and pendants.

Low-voltage MR-16 (mini-reflector)
Description. Tiny (2"-diameter) projector bulb; gives small circle of light from a distance.
Uses. Low-voltage track fixtures, mono-spots, and recessed downlights.

Low-voltage PAR
Description. Similar to auto headlight; tiny filament, shape, and coating give precise direction.
Uses. To project a small spot of light a long distance.

Storage

SHELF-CONSCIOUS CONTROLS TO END CONFUSION

A place for everything and everything in its place—it's an admirable adage that's a bit easier to remember than follow. But a variety of storage systems in a range of styles can help you corral clutter and display prized possessions. You can choose anything from simple shelves to storage walls tailored exactly to fit your needs.

Though expensive, built-ins allow you to customize your storage while maximizing available space. For instance, when you design a custom wall unit you can build all the way up to the ceiling. Painted the color of your walls and finished with matching trim, wall units blend in and take up mini-

mal visual space. If you prefer something less permanent, shop for modular units that can be assembled in different ways to accommodate varied storage needs and spaces.

Book storage

Books are useless unless they are easily accessible. A successful design brings as many volumes as is practical into the mainstream of daily life. If you have books languishing in boxes in a basement, attic, or closet, you may want to convert part of a multipurpose room into a library. If space is at a premium, spread books throughout the area in a number of small collections— cookbooks in or near the kitchen and

classics and current best-sellers in the seating area, for example.

One way to incorporate books as well as photos and other display items is with a built-in wall unit that has drawers and cupboards up to counter height for closed storage, then shallower, open shelves up to the ceiling. A sliding ladder affording access to top shelves lends an authentic library look.

Storage units can be both pretty and practical. This double-duty island separates the kitchen and dining areas from the great room's seating space while offering a convenient spot to store cookbooks and display both cooking utensils and decorative pottery.

Computer storage

As technology continues to introduce new tools, we must think creatively about spaces in which to house them. A computer needs a permanent home; it may be fairly new in our lives, but it is most definitely—in one form or another—here to stay.

When you're creating computer storage, remember to include space for printers, modems, external drives, manuals, disk files, and software boxes. Dedicating a separate space within your great room as a home office allows you to incorporate computer paraphernalia into built-in or modular units with drawers for files, shelves for books and manuals, and cabinets for office supplies. But if no separate space exists, even adding a telephone jack near a handy table, desk, or countertop makes it easy for a laptop user to plug into the Internet.

Media storage

Increasingly complex entertainment systems—including televisions, VCRs,

An Asian-inspired, multilevel modular system provides display space plus cabinets and drawers to keep miscellany tucked away.

stereo equipment, CDs, DVDs, video-tapes, movie screens, projectors, and remotes—require substantial, well-planned storage. If a television or monitor is to be concealed in a cabinet or enclosure, make sure the enclosure is well ventilated; heat buildup eventually kills transistors and printed circuits.

Remote-controlled, wide-screen, flat-panel televisions (some as thin as 2 inches) can hang on walls, under kitchen cabinets, or virtually anywhere. But any television can be removed from the traffic pattern if you place it near the ceiling, either on a shelf or suspended from a special bracket (available where sets are sold).

Requirements for a large-screen projection television depend on which type you have. The projecting equipment for a front-projection television

needs to be positioned directly in front of the screen, near the base or near the ceiling. The gear required for rear-projection models is concealed in the cabinet containing the screen.

Movie screens are typically installed from the ceiling to roll down as needed. Projectors can be hidden in a cabinet or installed on a shelf across the room.

Stereo components can be stacked, in or out of sight, in a custom audio tower, on a stereo rack, or in a piece of furniture adapted for the task, such as a desk or bookshelf. If you tackle the furniture conversion yourself, arrange components and peripherals according to their serial connection, then drill holes as necessary to lead cables and wires out the back to a heavy-duty outlet strip that's equipped with a surge protector. Use the ganglia model to organize wires and cables: play out just enough wire or cable to reach the required distance to a connection and then wrap the rest in on itself with a twist-tie or rubber band.

Freestanding shelf supports made of copper pipe create a vivid contemporary display wall with a whimsical space for the television set right in the middle.

Double-duty Furnishings

A MARRIAGE OF FORM AND FUNCTION

Sofas, chairs, tables, and storage cabinets can help organize activity areas and traffic patterns within a gathering place merely by their placement. Some of this versatile furniture, built-in or freestanding, serves several purposes. For example, a window seat tucked into an alcove off the kitchen lets people chat with the chef or curl up with a cookbook. Pullout drawers underneath the seat can store books, games, or even table linens.

Multifunctional furnishings

In an open-plan great room, a kitchen island performs many roles: work surface, casual dining spot, storage unit, and display area. Guests can convene around it without disturbing work in the kitchen. A properly designed island also effectively separates the kitchen from other areas.

Another hard-working paragon of versatility is a dining table. It's the gathering spot for eating, conversation, playing games, and doing homework. Depending on how it is positioned, the dining table can separate kitchen and eating areas from the seating area of a great room.

A sideboard's traditional use is for extra storage and display space in a dining room or kitchen; some styles even include a buffet surface. Depending on its height, it might also be tucked behind a sofa.

Occasional tables, such as long, narrow consoles, often are placed behind a sofa to hold a table lamp, books and magazines, drinks, or objets d'art. When the sofa cannot face the room's entrance, this arrangement makes an effective visual divider that appears more welcoming than the back of the sofa. A library table placed parallel to and out from a wall can subdivide a room as well as doing double duty as a console table and desk, with lamps for both ambient and task lighting. Low bookcases do double duty as space dividers, with a combination of open and closed shelves to provide display room on each side. Glass doors will keep books on open shelves free from dust and valuables safe from small hands.

Coffee tables are usually placed in front of sofas to provide a convenient space to rest books and magazines, drinks and snacks—and even feet. If you wouldn't dream of putting your feet up on a table, you might try an ottoman. This multipurpose piece also can be used for extra seating or, with a large tray on top, be transformed into a coffee table. Some ottomans open up to provide storage space for blankets, games, and toys, and some even convert into an extra bed for guests.

Similar in function and form, coffee tables and ottomans come in many shapes, from long and narrow to square

To make a seating area in a multipurpose room, pull furniture away from the walls and "float" it around a focal point, such as this fireplace. The oversize ottoman takes the place of a coffee table.

or round. If an ottoman is to be used primarily as a coffee table, it should be an inch or two higher than the seating. You can more easily enjoy its versatility by adding casters to the legs.

Armoires, having migrated from the bedroom, are now employed as handsome, useful storage for family rooms and other gathering places. These popular options can hold everything from books to video and audio equipment, providing maximum storage space while taking up minimal floor space. Some furniture companies manufacture an office-in-an-armoire suitable for a multifunctional room; you can conceal the contents simply by closing the doors.

Floating furnishings

Lining the walls of a seating area with furnishings is a conventional decorating approach. But this arrangement tends to

put an uncomfortable distance between people when they're seated and makes it difficult to divide an open plan into activity areas. "Floating" furnishings in the room (pulling them away from the walls) makes for a more intimate, convivial grouping; it also buys valuable space for bookcases and traffic.

The typical floating arrangement consists of a sofa and chairs positioned as a focal point to create an inner room. Furnishings that float need not be parallel to the walls. A sofa placed on the diagonal, across a corner, opens up a room. An area rug that's also on the diagonal strengthens and anchors the arrangement, but you can float seating diagonally even if the rug is parallel to the walls. Adding casters to chairs offers flexible seating possibilities, making it easy to change from one configuration to another.

Subtly blending home office elements into a family room makes the area perform dual duty. The computer and printer occupy space that once functioned as a wet bar (top left). Discreetly positioned under the skirts of the country French accent table (top right) is a two-drawer filing cabinet.

Personal Expressions

FINAL TOUCHES FOR INTEREST AND IDENTITY

A glance at the hub of your home, that informal place where your family comes together, shows not only how you live, but also who you are. Your family's identity and interests are revealed here more than in any other room in the house. The heirlooms, collectibles, paintings, favorite books, and other objects gathered in this comfortable space are meant not to impress but to express the owners' personalities.

Display guidelines

A casual approach usually reigns when it comes to displaying objects that the family truly enjoys. Wherever the eye falls when you enter a room or look from one room to another, on a table behind a sofa, on top of an armoire—these are all natural placements. Or accessories can be positioned where you want guests to look—by displaying a sculpture on a console table in the line of vision to a window wall, for example.

Designers have a few more formal guidelines, such as the "odd number rule," which recommends grouping an uneven number of pieces together; three to five is typical. Or try their formula "shiny, matte, tall, and fat." This means that, when combining accessories, you might include items that fit all these categories, such as tall shiny candlesticks, a favorite round vase, and grandmother's matte-finish plate.

Collections

What you choose to collect in life, whether it's cartoon lunch boxes, model cars, or antique teddy bears, reveals much about you—your passions, your experiences, even your sense of humor.

Anyone who loves literature will admire this Mission-style gathering place. Glass cabinet doors allow easy examination of book titles; a well-positioned table offers ample space for a snack or a story.

Because collections have such a personal significance, it's important to arrange them in ways that enhance their beauty or meaning.

The most successful arrangements look as though they were effortlessly composed. For maximum impact, consider clustering items. If they vary in size, layer them by placing shorter, smaller objects in front and taller, larger objects in back for a sense of depth. Show off small objects against a wall, on a shelf or tabletop, or on a windowsill. Large objects such as urns or wooden rocking horses can go on the floor, flanking a fireplace or grouped in a corner.

To achieve harmony within a grouping, choose pieces of different shapes and sizes but stick to a common color (verdigris pottery, for example) or material (such as pewter pieces).

Draw attention to three-dimensional works of art, such as a collection of

bowls, by silhouetting them against a plain background. If bowls are decorated inside, display them down low, perhaps on a coffee table.

Effective display always involves experimentation. Fortunately, collectibles are easy to rearrange, unlike major furnishings. To start afresh, remove the collection and study your room. Audition your favorite piece in different locations, then add others one by one. You'll quickly appreciate that objects can be used effectively in several spots.

You reveal who you are by the collections you display. Objets d'art (top left) are colorful indicators of the owner's interests. Chinese porcelains and orchids (top right) complement a library and music room. Seashells, books, glass, and pewter (right center) adorn bar shelves. False-front volumes (bottom right) hide a media room's videotapes.

design and photography credits

design

FRONT MATTER

1 Interior Design: Joan Osburn/ Osburn Design **2** Interior Design: Pacific Dimensions, Inc.; Architect: Bassenian/Lagoni Architects

ROOMS FOR ALL REASONS

4–5 Interior Design: Cynthia Brian/Starstyle Interiors & Design **6** Interior Design: Mike Hayden/

Master Remodelers **7 bottom** Interior Design: Barbara Jacobs/ Barbara Jacobs Interior Design; Lighting Design: Catherine Ng/Lightsmith's Design Group; Cabinets: Al Orozco **8** Interior Design: David Ramey **9** Interior Design: Kendall Wilkinson Design

DEFINING YOUR SPACE

10–11 Interior Design: Pamela Pennington/Tsun Yen Tang Wahab **12** Interior Design: S.E.A. Design/

Build **13** Interior Design: Giulietti/Associates **15** Interior Design: Marty Sears; Architect: Stephen Smith/Cooper, Johnson, Smith Architects, Inc. **17** Interior Design: Leezinski Design Associates; Architect: Doug Walter Architects **18** Interior Design: Amanda Knobel and Linda Miller/ Renaissance Interior Design **19** Architect: Rick Chesmore (Chesmore/Buck Architecture) **21 top** Interior Design: Donna Vining/Vining Design Associates **21 bottom** Architects: George Israel and Elaine Young **22** Architect: Richard Archer/ Overland Partners, Inc. **23** Interior Design: S.E.A. Design/Build **25** Interior Design: D. J. Lyon; Architect: Gayle McGregor **26** Interior Design: Linda S. Kaufman **27** Interior Design: Karen Graul; Kitchen Design: Kirk Craig; Architect: Kurt Archer **28** Lighting Design: Melinda Morrison Lighting Design; Architect: Byron Kuth, Liz Ranieri, and Doug Thornley (Kuth/Ranieri) **29** Interior Design: Cindy Zelazny Rodenhaver **30** Interior Design: Tony Cooper/Splinter Furniture Design **31 top** Interior Design: Marty Sears; Architect: Stephen Smith/Cooper, Johnson, Smith Architects, Inc. **31 bottom** Architect: Rick Chesmore (Chesmore/ Buck Architecture)

GREAT GATHERING PLACES

32–33 Interior Design: David Ramey **34–35** Interior Design: Surrey Interiors; Architect: J. Allen Sayles; Contractor: Da Silva Construction, Inc. **38–39** Interior

Design: David Dalton Associates, Inc. **40–41** Architect: James McCalligan **42–43** Interior Design: Creative Kitchen Designs, Woodgrain Woodworks, Greg Straub/Bay View Tile **44–45** Interior Design: Pacific Dimensions, Inc.; Architect: Bassenian/Lagoni Architects **46–47** Interior Design: Barbara Jacobs/Barbara Jacobs Interior Design **48–49** Interior Design: David Dalton Associates, Inc. **50–51** Interior Design: Lindsay Steenblock/County Clare Design; Architect: Robert Earl **52–53, 53 bottom** Interior Design: Claudia Fleury/Claudia's Designs **53 top** Architect: James McCalligan **54–55** Interior Design: Lindsay Steenblock/County Clare Design; Upholsterer: Peter Luzak/Master Craft Upholstery **57** Architect: Jimmy Tittle **58–59** Cabinets: Kevin Coy; Contractor/Builder: Peter Kyle **59 bottom** Interior Design: Jeff Shuler/Jeff Shuler & Associates **60–61** Interior Design: Leslie Harris/Leslie Harris Interiors **62** Interior Design: Lindsay Steenblock/County Clare Design **63** Interior Design: Jeff Shuler/Jeff Shuler & Associates **64–65** Architect: James McCalligan **67** Interior Design: Pacific Dimensions, Inc.; Architect: Bassenian/Lagoni Architects **68–69** Interior Design: Tres McKinney/Richard Witzel & Associates **70–71** Interior Design: Gigi Rogers Design **72–73** Interior Design: Marilyn Riding Design **74–75** Interior Design: Sandy Bacon/Sandy Bacon Design Group; Home Theater: John Maxon/Integrated

System Design; Cabinets: Heartwood Studio **76–77** Barbara Jacobs/Barbara Jacobs Interior Design **78–79** Interior Design: Bobbie Frohman Interior Design **80–81** Interior Design: Lavi Forte, Inc. **82–83** Interior Design: Lorenzo Petroni and Maria Elena Petroni Interiors; Architect: James McCalligan **84** Interior Design: Lindsay Steenblock/County Clare Design **85 bottom** Architect: James McCalligan **86** Interior Design: David Ramey **87** Interior Design: Pacific Dimensions, Inc.; Architect: Bassenian/Lagoni Architects **88–89** Interior Design: Donald Clement and Bob Powers; Architect: Donald Clement and Jim McCalligan **90** Interior Design: J. Hettinger Interiors **91** Interior Design: Miller/Stein; Architect: Robert Mittelstadt **92–93** Interior Design: Leslie Gamblin **94** Interior Design: Dianne Adams; Window Treatment: Mary's Custom Workroom **95** Interior Design: Jeff Shuler/Jeff Shuler & Associates **96–97** Architect: Rei Tanimoto and Earl Gorton **98–99** Interior Design: Jennifer Bevan Interiors **100–101** Interior Design: Barbara Jacobs/Barbara Jacobs Interior Design; Architect: Kenzo Handa/Kenzo Handa Architecture; Contractor: Lars Elmengard Construction; Furniture Fabricator: Sas Quinn Furniture **102–103** Architect: Randolph Finn **104–105** Architect: James McCalligan

DESIGN ELEMENTS

108 Interior Design: Joan Osburn/Osburn Design

109 top Interior Design: Steven Harby **109 bottom** Interior Design: Sandra C. Watkins; Paint Color and Fabrics: Joan Osburn/Joan Osburn Design **110 top** Interior Design: Taylor Woodrow **110 bottom** Interior Design: Ann Jones Interiors **111 (1)** Barbara Magee and Ann Johnson/Custom House Furniture **111 (2)** Concrete Tile Designer: Dagney Alda Steinsdottir/Alda Designs **111 (3)** Interior Design: Gordon Phaby/Sechrist Design **111 (4)** Interior Design: Roberta Brown Root **113** Interior Design: Frank Van Duerm Design Associates **114** Architect: Backen, Aragoni & Ross **115 top** Architect: Bredthauer/Curran & Associates **115 bottom** Interior Design: Barbara Jacobs/Barbara Jacobs Interior Design; Architect: Kenzo Handa/Kenzo Handa Architecture; Shoji Screens: Jimmy Miakawa/Japan Woodworking **116** Interior Design: Kay Heizman **117** Interior Design: Tres McKinney/Laura Ashley **118** Interior Design: Lynnette Reed and Marian Wheeler **119** Interior Design: Barbara Jacobs/Barbara Jacobs Interior Design **120** Architect: Ted Wengren **121 top** Interior Design: Barbara Jacobs/Barbara Jacobs Interior Design; Cabinets: Al Orozco **121 bottom** Interior Design: Wayne Palmer **123** Design/Contractor: R. J. Reedy Construction **125 top right** Interior Design: Helaine Moyse; Floral Design: Patrick Tandy **125 middle right** Interior Design: Monty Collins Interior Design **125 bottom right** Interior Design: Amanda Knobel and Linda Miller/Renaissance Interior Design

BACK MATTER

126 Interior Design: Alison Lufkin/Sullivan & Company, San Francisco **127** Interior Design: Pacific Dimensions, Inc.; Architect: Bassenian/Lagoni Architects

photography

Unless otherwise credited, all photographs are by **E. Andrew McKinney.**

Russell Abraham: 116, 118; **Alda Designs:** 111 (2); **Patrick Barta:** 19, 31 bottom; **Laurie Black:** 13 both; **Frederic Choisel:** 30; **J. Curtis:** 17 both; **Mark Darley/Esto:** 108; **Laurey W. Glenn:** 29; **Ken Gutmaker:** 12, 23 both, 110 bottom, 111 (3), 125 top left, 126; **Jamie Hadley:** 1, 9, 109 bottom, 111 (1), 123 all; **Philip Harvey:** 28, 38–39 all, 40–41 all, 53 top, 60, 61, 64–65 all, 80–81 all, 98–99 all, 110 top, 115 top; **Douglas Johnson:** 78–79 all, 90; **David Duncan Livingston:** 56, 91 bottom, 106–107, 122, 125 center; **Sylvia Martin:** 15, 22, 31 top; **Emily Minton:** 21 bottom, 25 both, 27 both, 57 both, 125 top right; **Rob Muir:** 21 top; **Gary W. Parker:** 114; **Tom Rider:** 85 top; **Michael Skott:** 111 (4), 112 bottom left; **SPC Photo Collection:** 18, 124 bottom right; **TimStreet-Porter/beateworks.com:** 109 top; **Brian Vanden Brink:** 120, 124; **David Wakely:** 121 bottom; **Greg West:** 26; **Eric Zepeda:** 10–11

index

Numbers in **bold face type** refer to photographs.